# Courageous Fathers of the Bible

## A Bible Study for Men

Joel Biermann

CONCORDIA PUBLISHING HOUSE · SAINT LOUIS

Copyright © 2011 Concordia Publishing House
3558 S. Jefferson Ave., St. Louis, MO 63118-3968
1-800-325-3040 • www.cph.org

Written by Joel Biermann

This publication may be available in braille, in large print, or on cassette tape for the visually impaired. Please allow 8 to 12 weeks for delivery. Write to Lutheran Blind Mission, 7550 Watson Road, St. Louis, MO 63119-4409; call toll-free 1-888-215-2455; or visit the Web site: www.blindmission.org.

1 2 3 4 5 6 7 8 9 10          20 19 18 17 16 15 14 13 12 11

# Contents

# Introduction

Fatherhood is under attack. You already know that. Given contemporary Western culture's obsession with diminishing and trivializing men in general—and fathers in particular—time does not need to be wasted making the case again. (If you doubt, simply observe the portrayal of each in popular media.) Suffice it to say that strong yet humble men, who take seriously their responsibility to raise pious and righteous children and who wield the ability to judge their world according to God's Word, are not encouraged by the forces at work around us. It would seem men like this are a threat to be tamed. And the campaign to tame them has been wildly successful.

This book is one small contribution to the effort to resist this assault. It aims to help these harried men recognize and embrace with zeal the sacred responsibility given to them when they entered into fatherhood. This study makes no pretense at being exhaustive in its treatment of the subject. It is not a textbook or the product of academic research. It is a series of reflections springing from the lives of real men. Highly selective and somewhat idiosyncratic, it hopefully presents a clear and witty picture of what the work of fatherhood is supposed to look like. The source is the Bible. More specifically, the source is the men whose stories are told in the Bible.

There is nothing particularly significant about the selection of biblical men to be considered. Most of the names are familiar, and their inclusion seems almost obvious. How could a book about biblical fathers not include Adam or Abraham or David? Certainly, many other men might have been included on the list, but the twelve in this volume are quite sufficient for the present project. Each one allows the consideration of some aspect of the responsibility of fatherhood.

It is important, though, to note that the lessons presented were not first determined and then the list of biblical men selected. This is not an example of an agenda in search of a supporting text. Indeed, there are probably many topics that could be critical to successful parenting that are not mentioned in these pages. And some of the discussions that animate the studies in this book might seem to some to be tangential or even irrelevant to the work of fatherhood.

The direction for this book and the individual studies within it came from the texts themselves—from the fathers themselves. We learn from Isaac what Isaac has to teach—regardless what others may consider to be lessons that are more vital, interesting, or relevant. And it is hoped within the process, these men will teach us lessons whose value and significance will surprise, challenge, and delight.

Some might be skeptical about the ability of the ancestral fathers of faith to speak to the needs of twenty-first-century men. While such skepticism may be excused, it is unfounded. Much has changed with the passing of millennia, but the human condition and the realities of familial interaction are essentially unchanged. People are still people. Interpersonal issues and conflict are not fundamentally different today than they were in the days of the patriarchs. The problems that perplexed Jacob or Solomon continue to afflict fathers today. These ancient fathers and their ancient challenges are startlingly familiar. They have much to teach us.

Of course, each man included in this book is a unique individual. They are real men, not representative figures or symbols of every man. Their stories are quite different as they face assorted circumstances from the perspective of their widely divergent personalities and character. We would not expect David to respond to situations the same way that Noah would. But even this notion raises another problem—we usually don't know very much about these men, and so it is difficult to know just what Noah would or wouldn't do. An effort must be made, then, not to indulge in too much speculation. Still, the stories provide information enough, and insights can be gained without resorting to creative reading of the texts.

Since the men considered in the following pages are real men, they have unique stories, but they also share a common story. In fact, virtually every one of the chapters in this book could be that same story: a man of God striving to do things God's way, falling flat on his face in the process, and learning to live in the grace of forgiveness. The degree of failure varies, of course, but failure is always present. So, these men have lessons to offer by virtue of their successes and positive examples, but they can also teach by way of negative examples. Sometimes those applications are the most powerful and poignant of all. Dickens put the words in the mouth of Ebenezer Scrooge as he tried to dissuade the Spirit of Christmas Past from exiting the window with him in tow. " 'I am mortal,' Scrooge pleaded, 'and liable to fall.' " Indeed, this is the ultimate story of every man. We are all mortal and liable to fall. So, reading and studying the stories of those who tried and fell can only aid us in our own striving.

Finally, it needs to be acknowledged that the goal motivating and shaping the twelve sketches that make up this book is neither exegetical exactitude nor homiletical originality or inspiration. The author is qualified for neither enterprise. Rather, the chapters are simple reflections with an intentional aim at practicality. Don't fear, the interpretation is sound and founded on solid theological presuppositions, but the consistent objective is the application of God's lively Word to the real lives of God's people. By God's grace, His truth will be evident: insight and inspiration for the task of fatherhood and delightful declaration and delivery of His extraordinary Gospel.

The book is written and formatted with a men's Bible study group in mind. However, groups that are not made up exclusively of men will also find the studies to be of keen interest and value. Neither should individuals shy from taking up the book and reading it either slowly as a study or at a single sitting. God's truth speaks in manifold settings. However it is used, every reader is encouraged not to overlook the answers in the Leader Guide, as many ideas and thoughts gleaned from the texts are introduced or expanded in these discussions.

# Suggestions for Small-Group Participants

1. As a courtesy to others, arrive on time.

2. Before you begin, spend some time in prayer, asking God to strengthen your faith through a study of His Word. The Scriptures were written so that we might believe in Jesus Christ and have life in His name (John 20:31).

3. Be an active participant. The leader will guide the group's discussion, not give a lecture.

4. Avoid dominating the conversation by answering every question or by giving unnecessarily long answers. On the other hand, avoid the temptation to not share at all.

5. Treat anything shared in your group as confidential until you have asked for and received permission to share it outside of the group. Treat information about others outside of your group as confidential until you have asked for and received permission to share it with group members.

6. Some participants may be new to Bible study or new to the Christian faith. Help them feel welcome and comfortable.

7. Affirm other participants when you can. If someone offers what you perceive to be a "wrong" answer, ask the Holy Spirit to guide him to seek the correct answer from God's Word.

8. Keep in mind that the questions are discussion starters. Don't be afraid to ask additional questions that relate to the topic. Don't get the group off track.

9. If you are comfortable doing so, volunteer now and then to pray at the beginning or end of the session.

# Adam

There is, apparently, some debate over what qualifies as the shortest poem in the English language. Some claim that it is simply:

I
Why?

Others contend for:

Me
We

But, the traditional favorite, and perhaps more orthodox poem (since it does not rely on the title to supply part of the rhyme and rhythm) is titled variously "On the Antiquity of Microbes" or sometimes, simply, "Fleas." It seems reasonable in light of the present topic to suggest yet another (and even briefer) title for the same, but differently titled, epic poem. In which case, the title and poem would be:

Kids
Adam had 'em.

Quite rightly, Adam will always be remembered first for his role as the progenitor of the human race. He is *the* first man. The name *Adam* evokes immediate thoughts of Eve, the garden, and the beginning of things. Adam is man number one. But, not only is Adam the first man, he is also the first father—which is, on reflection, somewhat obvious: no fatherhood, no human race! The fact that we are all here is evidence of Adam's success at fatherhood.

What we know about Adam's vocation as father is, truthfully, almost nothing. The scriptural account in the Book of Genesis is characteristically brief and lacking in even the most basic elaboration. Actually, this phenomenon is more common than one might expect in the pages of the Bible. So often, a biblical story is told with only the bare facts supplied, and we are left to wonder about the more human and relational side of the story—the part of the story left out. So it is in the story of Adam and his fatherhood: "Now Adam knew Eve his wife, and she conceived and bore Cain." That's the way it is told in Genesis 4:1, and that's about it for the biblical account of the fatherhood of Adam. All right, there *is* a bit more.

Verse 2 adds, "Again, she bore his brother Abel." And a few verses later we learn about Seth and other sons and daughters of Adam. What we don't know about Adam is what kind of father he was. We don't know how he felt when he and Eve welcomed their first son into the world and they experienced the fulfillment of God's promise to them. We don't know what kind of influence he had on his sons or what concerns he had for them. Was he aware of a simmering sibling rivalry that would end in fratricide? Did he see in Cain character traits that made him lose sleep and wrestle with ways to reach his troubled firstborn son? Of course, it would be easy enough to speculate about all of these interesting questions and supply reasonable—or better yet, fanciful—answers. But the Bible is frustratingly silent about such speculation. Obviously, the Holy Spirit considered other issues to be more significant and worthy of attention than the feelings of Adam or the sort of fatherhood that he practiced. We are left to wonder.

We can also wonder about Adam as a man. It is important to remember that while Adam has the singular distinction of being *the* first man, he was still a man. That is, he was not some sort of mythical "everyman" meant to stand for all men. He was not a dispassionate ideal prototype man devoid of individual personality and character. Adam was a bona fide real man. He had a unique personality. He had quirks and habits—and given the fallen nature of both he and his wife, these were no doubt irksome to Eve on occasion! Adam was a man with all the wonderful strengths and liabilities common to all men, but he displayed them in a way that was all his own—just like any other man has his own way of doing things. Adam had a way of talking with his sons. He had a way of going about the day's work and a way of greeting his wife in the morning. He had a sense of humor that was his very own. He was a real man. But, again, the account in Genesis tells us nothing about any of this. What kind of man he was is unknown to us. Still, it is good to think of Adam as a real man, and to appreciate the sort of challenges and heartaches and delights that would have filled his life and provided opportunity for the formation and display of his own peculiar personality.

While it would be fascinating to know more about Adam as a man and a father (it is undeniably tempting to suggest a portrait to compensate for what is not provided), it would be a perilous and foolhardy project. It is never a good idea to guess about and fill in what Scripture leaves blank. It is probably wisest, then, to give more thought to what can be known with confidence about Adam, and to explore the lessons to be learned in this regard a bit more.

What we know with certainty is that Adam was doing what he had been created to do. Having sons and daughters was the responsibility that he had been given back in chapter 1 of Moses' first book. Right after God had created Adam in His own image, He blessed the first couple and gave them the familiar charge: "Be fruitful and multiply and fill the earth and subdue it and have dominion over the fish of the sea and over the birds of the heavens and over every living thing that moves on the earth" (Genesis 1:28).

Quite rightly, this has been designated the "first Great Commission." The term reminds us of the solemnity of the charge and also of the duration of the charge. Genesis 1:28 provides the raison d'être of Adam—it spells out Adam's reason for being. He is put into the garden, into the creation, to take care of it. He is responsible for it. He is not to pillage the creation or to ravage it for his own purposes. He is to look after, protect, and steward the creation. This mandate is, obviously, extraordinarily significant because it applies not only to the first man, but to every heir of Adam as well. It is the raison d'être for every man. Man lives to care for the creation. This is a subject worthy of significant exploration and reflection, and carries immediate implications for a wealth of environmental and creation-care questions and topics that are of critical importance for Adam's twenty-first-century descendants. This discussion, however, lies beyond our immediate concern. For now, it is the first, and too easily overlooked, part of the First Great Commission that is of interest to us.

The Creator specifically commands Adam and Eve to "be fruitful and multiply and fill the earth" (Genesis 1:28). In other words, the first couple was to get busy and have children. God's desire and first instruction to Adam after marriage was for Adam to be a father. Adam was supposed to have kids. So, when Adam had them, he was being obedient to God's will. When Adam became a father, he was doing what God had created him to do. Adam was created to become a father. Adam had his answer to the "I Why?" question. His task was to be a father. Certainly the command has direct meaning for Adam's heirs, as well. No doubt there are some who would limit this command to Adam, since for the first man the need for population expansion was evident. And others might argue that the mandate has been met with great success, and more than enough descendants of Adam and Eve have been produced to "fill the earth." Still others might empty the first Great Commission of its significance by tying its meaning to ancient Semitic culture and values, which by implication no longer apply to sophisticated twenty-first-century men.

But every one of these stances simply amounts to an attempt to deflect and dilute the thrust of God's defining instruction to Adam and his progeny. Biblical interpreters can debate the meaning and best understanding of the proto-commandment, but for those who seek to live within the plan established by the Creator, the point of the passage is clear: fatherhood is a good thing and has the blessing of God. It is good and right to be a father. It is good and right to invest in the raising of children—which is inherent in the task of filling the earth with wise and capable offspring.

This point should not be passed over too quickly or shrugged off as self-evident and unworthy of further comment. In fact, in the world that we inhabit, it certainly is not assumed that men are, first and foremost, put here to be fathers. Indeed, there is no shortage of alternative goals, purposes, and aspirations that men are urged to choose and pursue at the expense of the fatherhood mandate. Attitudes and societal emphases change with the passage of the decades, of course. And the importance placed on fatherhood is perhaps higher now than it was in recent time past. Still, the idea that a man's most important task and highest aspiration should be the raising of children would probably strike most men as strange—or just plain wrong. Men have more important things to do than to get distracted with raising kids. There are careers to build, skills to hone, sports to watch, diversions to be pursued, riches to be gained, houses to be built, personal dreams to be fulfilled, and pleasures to be treasured.

Certainly, men have many legitimate and valuable pursuits, and the obligation to subdue the earth takes on many different forms. It is good that men continue to find productive and meaningful avenues in which to invest themselves in the task of caring for the creation—even when his investment in the creation may not be as obvious and immediately tangible as Adam pruning a fig tree or harvesting a crop of olives. Still, even these good pursuits must not be allowed to usurp the pride of place that should be given to fatherhood.

The problem in our culture is not that men are opting out of marriage and fatherhood. For most men, the desire to join in the venture of marriage and the drive to procreate is inescapable and will not be denied. This irresistible drive to fatherhood is a product of God's natural law that permeates all creation and thus every man, but that is another topic for another time.

Nevertheless, simply having kids—for whatever reason—does not guarantee the fulfillment of the mandate of the first commission. St. Paul famously clarifies the task of fatherhood in his letter to the Ephesians: "Fathers, do not provoke your children to anger, but bring them up in the discipline and instruction of the Lord" (Ephesians 6:4).

Unlike some members of the animal kingdom, a man has not discharged his parental obligation simply by providing half of the necessary DNA, and then departing in search of the next interesting thing. Nor has he met his responsibility by giving his children the proverbial roof over their heads and food on the table, nor even by putting them through college free of the student loan burden. It is not sufficient, then, to get married and have kids. The kids must be raised God's way. The kids must be brought up to be contributing and capable members of the world. This is no easy task. It will not be accomplished by ranking fatherhood tasks behind career, hobbies, and cherished personal diversions and activities. The task requires the continual investment of self. The task demands sacrifice of personal desires and favorite pastimes.

The task is unrelenting in its expectations. The task is far greater than any man realizes when he first gets the news about his entry into the wonderful and surprisingly challenging world of fatherhood. It is a sacred task, one that comes directly from God.

To be a father is to be charged with one of the most important works of a lifetime, second only to being a husband. For those men whom God has called to the vocation of husband and father, loving his wife and raising his children so that they know God's mercy, truth, and purposes are high and holy callings.

It all comes down to a right understanding of *vocation*. This is the term used by the reformers, and one that captures well the "God-givenness" of the work we have to do. For too long in the history of the Christian Church, the important concept of vocation was forgotten or reduced to a caricature of what it is meant to be. Vocation is not merely career. Vocation is certainly not to be equated with full-time service in a church career. Vocation is not the things you are "good at." Vocation is the purpose that directs your living. Vocation is the obligation that has been given to you to fulfill. Vocation is God's instruction and guide for how you are to use your time, your abilities, and your wisdom. Vocation is meant to define your life, and so vocation becomes critical in one's self-understanding.

In recent years, vocation has been receiving more attention in scholarly circles, and the truths of this wonderful biblical idea have been trickling down for the benefit of all. It is the truth that reverberates through the opening chapters of the Bible as we hear the story of Adam. The first Great Commission was the giving of vocation to Adam. Broad and general in scope, the commission of chapter 1 became altogether specific for Adam. He was given a wife to love—a vocation. He was given Cain, Abel, Seth, and many other sons and daughters—a vocation. Of course, he was given a garden to tend, and then ground on which to toil—a vocation. That same general commission directs your own life, and then finds expression in all the specific vocations that shape your days: son, husband, father, employee, neighbor, citizen. You have tasks given to you by God. You have tasks that only you can do.

Of course, it is quite true that a man typically knows several vocations for which he is responsible. And it is also true that at times the obligations of any two or more vocations may conflict. What it takes to accomplish one vocation very well may interfere with the successful fulfillment of another important vocation. This is reality in our post-Eden world. But the singular importance of the role of father, as it was given to Adam and then reinforced by St. Paul, helps to clarify the best way to resolve those quandaries of colliding vocations. While every true vocation is a gift and an obligation from the hand of God—and so it will, obviously, conform to the will of God as revealed in His Law—not every vocation is equally important. Certainly a man's relationship with God through repentant faith in Jesus Christ comes first, then a husband's duties to his wife, then a father's obligation to his children, and so on.

A good guide in thinking about the best way to reconcile conflicting vocational demands is to consider the vocations you have been given that no one else can do. It is likely that another man could be found to do what you do to earn a paycheck. But, as long as you live, your wife has only one man available to be husband to her. And, God has given your children only one man to be their father. The work may not be glamorous in the eyes of the world. It is too often done without any apparent compensation or benefit. It does not matter. How you feel about that work is irrelevant. The work you have been given to do is holy work. The vocation of father is a sacred vocation.

This world, and this world's families, need men who are willing to embrace the holy work of fatherhood. It is a sacred charge. It is noble and honorable work. Few things matter more than being a father who invests in the task of living out his vocation. We know all that we need to know about Adam. He was given his vocation, his specific work that God had called him to do. You have been given your vocation—the work that God has put you here to do. Don't let anything keep you from doing it.

## Questions

1. Is the legacy of Adam positive or negative? What comes to mind when you think about Adam?

2. What details or insights do you wish the biblical text had included in the narrative about Adam?

3. Read Genesis 5:3. What is the significance of Seth being singled out as Adam's son? Why not Cain or Abel?

4. Of Adam's three sons, which one seemed to be most like his father? Why do you think this?

5. How does the tragedy of the fall, recorded in Genesis 3, impact the meaning and significance of the First Great Commission? How might the very fact that Adam chooses to become a father be a demonstration of courage?

6. What vocations are you responsible to fulfill at this time in your life? How does seeing them as God-given affect your attitude toward them or the way that you do them?

7. What do you think are some of the pressures and ideas that work against a man being able to see fatherhood as a primary vocation?

8. How might it demand courage from a man simply to be a father who takes seriously his responsibility to raise his children in the discipline and instruction of the Lord?

9. Much of the Adam story is rather grim and leaves a stark and challenging picture of fatherhood. Is this fair and accurate? How does the famous promise of Genesis 3:15 fit into this understanding of fatherhood?

10. Of all the lessons that Adam has to teach us, what is the one key thought that you will take with you into the week ahead? How will you put this into action?

# Noah

Noah knew something about family togetherness. He had no choice. No doubt, Noah also knew something about the pros and cons of vacationing with extended family members. Had Noah kept a journal of his life, or even a much briefer journal about his experience with the ark, almost certainly it would have contained a wealth of valuable insights into the dynamics of family systems and interrelationships.

Noah, his wife, three sons—each with his own wife—and a menagerie of animals of the greatest conceivable variety were confined together in a floating stable roughly the size of one and a half football fields for a year and ten days. Indeed, Noah knew something about family togetherness—no doubt he knew something about a great many other things as well. Ship building, food storage and preservation, animal husbandry, monotony management, Noah was an expert in them all. It is a pity that he did not leave a journal—of course, having been penned by a man, even if it were discovered, this imaginary journal might not be as helpful or insightful as we would like:

Day 23: Rain. Fed and watered animals. Cleaned lower deck.
Day 113: Sunny. Fed and watered animals. Still floating.
Day 303: Partly sunny. Fed and watered animals. Still sitting on the mountain.

Who could expect a guy—even one with five hundred-plus years of experience with the complexities of life—to explore the dark labyrinth of his own emotions? Who could expect him to reflect on the dynamics at work among the eight men and women sharing the space and the work of the animal-laden ark? He probably didn't even notice that there were interpersonal dynamics at work. Why would he? There was work to be done. Why waste time with things he did not understand? Although his wife may very well have alerted Noah to the need to notice such things. But alas, we are sliding rapidly toward speculation with its inherent hazards. What we know is enough. Noah was a dad, and Noah gives evidence of remarkable courage.

Using the adjective *courageous* to describe Noah is hardly a novel or daring suggestion. Of the great patriarchs of Genesis, Noah is probably the leading candidate to be coupled with the virtue of courage. We think immediately of pious Noah living in a debauched world of violence and excess and imagine his courage to stand for morality and decency when everyone else was celebrating what is decadent and evil. One can hardly exaggerate the depths of wickedness to which the earth's inhabitants had descended. Things were bad—bad enough to provoke the wrath and curse of God. "The LORD saw that the wickedness of man was great in the earth, and that every intention of the thoughts of his heart was only evil continually" (Genesis 6:5).

Things were so far gone that the Creator's only acceptable solution was to wipe out virtually every living thing and start over. But there, in the middle of the mess, is Noah. Noah "found favor in the eyes of the LORD" (Genesis 6:8). Indeed, he found favor because Noah was a man apart. "Noah was a righteous man, blameless in his generation" (Genesis 6:9). In fact, Noah was one of the handful of scriptural characters described with the breathtaking, wonderful, and simple sentence: "Noah walked with God" (Genesis 6:9). Incredible. Living like that in a world like that took courage.

Before we tread too far down that path, though, it might be wise to check the text. All the books and film representations of Noah notwithstanding, the account in Genesis says nothing about Noah's neighbors or about any exchanges between the patriarch and those who lived next door. Such potential meetings are excellent fodder for our imaginations, of course. We love to picture the men and women of Noah's clan laboring on the ark and its provisions, while neighbors gawk and mock at the folly of building a monstrosity of a boat, presumably on dry land far from any body of water. But the biblical record is silent on this point. The space between God's directive to Noah and the time that all the passengers embarked for their voyage is covered by a single verse: "Noah did this; he did all that God commanded him" (Genesis 6:22).

Three words in English present a lesson that most of us perpetually struggle to learn much less practice. God gave a command and Noah responded: "Noah did this." No discussion. No clarification. No deliberation. God commanded and Noah did. While others may call it courage or dogged determination, what's clear is that Noah's God-given faith had yielded the fruit of obedience. God had chosen Noah for a reason: Noah believed, and thus Noah obeyed.

*Righteous* is a big, loaded word. It is not used lightly. Christians hear the word *righteous* and hear "sinless, and worthy of God's praise." And since we have been taught, and taught quite rightly, that no one is perfect, that no one is righteous (Romans 3:23), we are taken aback by the description of Noah as righteous. This deserves a closer look, then. We need to understand what it meant that Noah was righteous, because when that is understood, the real courage of Noah the patriarch, Noah the father, will be understood.

It is true, of course, that *righteous* is a "God-word." It is used to describe a person who is able to stand before God without fear of incurring God's wrath. And when the word is used in this context— and this is probably the typical religious context—then the message of the Christian Church needs to ring loudly in our ears: no one is righteous. The only righteous ones are those who have received God's forgiveness delivered for the sake of the life, death, and resurrection of God's Son, Jesus. No one earns the designation of righteous. It must be given. This is absolutely, categorically true.

Thus, when it came to his relationship with God, Noah was righteous, but not because he had earned that designation. He was righteous the same way that you are righteous—only by God-given faith, which trust in God made possible; faith that clung to God's promise. "Noah did this" did not make Noah righteous before God. Noah's obedience was merely one manifestation of Noah's righteousness that had a source other than his deeds or convictions. Noah was righteous because he relied on God, and God alone, to make his righteousness a reality.

In another sense, though, with regard to Noah's relationship with the rest of the world around him, it is quite possible to determine that Noah was righteous simply in light of the fact that he was living the way that he was supposed to live. This is civil righteousness. It does not and cannot aid a man to be righteous before God. It does not save. Noah was doing what he had been created to do. He was doing what God had put him in the world to do. He was being a human according to the will and plan of God. Noah was following God's will, he was obeying God's Law. So, in the eyes of the world, and by the standards of the world— conformity to the rules built into the fabric of the world itself— Noah was righteous. He was a man who was living the way he was supposed to live. This fact was all the more apparent in the context of the debased and decaying world in which Noah found himself. This is what Moses meant when he introduced Noah: "Noah was a righteous man, blameless in his generation" (Genesis 6:9).

Noah was righteous, in this sense and in this context, because of what he was doing and not doing. He was unlike the rest. He was living obedient to God's will. He was righteous—not perfect (of course not!) and worthy of God's grace or salvation—but righteous in the sense of being upright and doing what God had put him here to do.

So, Noah is righteous in two ways. He is righteous before God by his faith and trust in the promise of God and his reliance on the provision of God. And, he is righteous before all creation, before his fellow men, by virtue of his exemplary living and fulfillment of his God-given purpose. The latter kind of righteousness took courage, no doubt. But, it is the former righteousness, the righteousness before his God and Maker, where Noah's courage is of most of interest.

Faith is a gift that man cannot conjure or keep by himself. It is also true that while the Holy Spirit does it all, the man who believes does the believing. Yes, you're right, it doesn't make much sense to say that it is both ways, but that is the reality of how faith works. God gives it and sustains it, and man does it. The new man created by God receives the gift of faith. And to live in faith is not easy. Indeed, it takes courage. This is the legacy of Noah that deserves careful consideration and emulation.

Lest we get caught up in the action and wonder of the story's plot and miss the real lesson of Noah and his ark, it is necessary to stop and consider the courage Noah displayed—not in building an ark, but in living in a state of absolute humility and dependence on God and God's promises. That's the marvelous part of this story.

Critics of the Bible's narrative about Noah and the flood find plenty to ridicule and dismiss as beyond credulity by virtue of the account of the stabled animals and the floodwater and its worldwide extent. "Impossible and ridiculous!" they declare with smug confidence. But, in their preoccupation with the details of the ark and the flood, they are oblivious to the part of the story that is actually the most astounding—the part that stuns anyone who gives it a moment's thought. The incredible thing is that surrounded by a sea of human wretchedness and self-serving sin, Noah was living righteous before God. Noah lived in the reality of simple trust, relying on God for everything. Noah lived dependent on God—dependent, utterly at the mercy of God, completely incapable of doing anything on his own—this was Noah's way of living. He knew what it meant to be a creature. Such willing, humble dependence on God is rare indeed. Noah exemplified it.

There is no better picture of Noah's position of abject dependence on God than Genesis 7:16. Everyone is on the ark: Noah, his wife, three sons and their wives, and a literal boatload of animals. The last animal has climbed aboard, and then verse 16: "Those that entered, male and female of all flesh, went in as God had commanded him. And the LORD shut him in."

God was taking care of Noah. Noah depends on God for everything—even to be the one to close the door and seal the occupants in their ship of salvation.

So, what does all of this have to do with fatherhood? Well, as you might expect, everything. Righteousness is the very heart of fatherhood. This is true of both dimensions of righteousness. It is certainly the case that a good father needs to be a man righteous in the eyes of the world—or even more importantly, righteous in the eyes of his own family. Sons and daughters, not to mention his wife, need to look at the man called husband and father and see a man who strives to live rightly, doing what God put him here to do (his vocation!), and doing it with consistency and commitment. A good father needs this.

But, even more, a good father needs to know what it means to be right before God. He needs to know what it means to live in absolute dependence on God for absolutely everything. A man who lives with this knowledge gives to his family a gift that defies calculation. He gives them the gift of a living example of faith.

By his living and his trusting, he presents his children with a picture of what it means to be fully human, what it means to live in total dependence on God. And as we clearly see in the case of Noah, this does not make one a wimp or a self-deprecating, incompetent, weak, timid, cowardly bystander in life. It makes a man such as Noah. That is the legacy of Noah. He was righteous. He was *right* before the world by deed, and he was *right* before God by faith. And his sons saw this—intimately and daily, they saw this.

We are not told much about how Noah raised his three sons or how he sought to influence them and their families. Actually, we are not told anything about this. But we can be relatively confident in assuming that Noah's righteousness was not lost on his children. Such righteous living is quite unique. Living as one who is completely dependent on God is hardly commonplace. And we can be quite certain that Noah would have approached his child-rearing just as he did everything else in life—in righteousness. That is, he would have done all that he could to be the best father possible, keeping his vocation of father at the front of his thinking and acting; and with regard to the other dimension of righteousness, living in complete dependence on God to provide all that was needed. Noah would have raised Shem, Ham, and Japheth clinging to the promises of God. That was how Noah lived. This is what it means to be a righteous father. Perfection has nothing to do with it. Noah made mistakes. (There is that awkward incident when Noah over-indulged in the fruit of his newly planted vineyard [Genesis 9:20–28].) Somehow, Noah's own righteous way of living did not find residence in the lives of all his sons. Ham and his progeny became the subject of a curse. Nevertheless, Noah was righteous. He was God's kind of man. He was God's kind of father.

God calls men to penitent faith. God calls men to repent when they are not perfect Christians, husbands, or fathers. He calls a man to be faithful . . . to do what he has been put here to do. This is what Noah did. And, at the same time, God calls a man to live before him in humble trust and in willing reliance on his giving and grace for everything. That is how Noah lived. That is how Noah functioned as a father.

God still calls men to do the same. The mark of a father who is doing things the right way, God's way, is righteousness. The righteous man is a man of integrity, who strives to fulfill his responsibilities with consistency. The righteous man is a man of faith who looks to God and trusts him for everything. This second, other aspect of righteousness is a vital component of faithful fatherhood. Living like this takes courage. It is not easy. It means trusting God to work through you, even when you are not sure about what you are doing. It means clutching to the promises of God when there is precious little evidence that he is paying any attention at all to what is going on in your home or hearing any of your prayers. It means doggedly following God's will in spite of the resistance you get from all the wise and sometimes well-meaning advisors who surround you and happily "help" you. It means living in confidence that dark days are not without end, and that the ark of your home will not drift forever. God will intervene. He will bring rest. The courageous father counts on God to do what God has promised to do.

It is too bad that Noah did not leave behind a ship's log for his days on the ark. It would have made for entertaining reading ... well, maybe. But what Noah *did* leave is even better. Noah left a legacy of righteousness. He demonstrated in vivid lessons what it means to take God at His word and do what one has been given to do. "Noah was a righteous man" (Genesis 6:9). Indeed. So are all who walk in his ways.

## Questions

1. Of all the animals that migrated to the ark for a year of cruising with Noah's family, which, do you think, posed the greatest challenge to Noah and his sons?

2. Read Genesis 6:5–22. What stands out to you? Based only on this text, what impression do you get of Noah's character?

3. The text emphasizes that the world and its men had become "filled with violence" (vv. 11 and 13). Is it surprising that this was the world's sin? Why would violence be singled out as corrupt and evil?

4. Why is it important to understand *righteousness* in two ways, or according to two dimensions? How does this view help to clarify the story of Noah?

5. Noah was righteous before God because of what God had done. How does a right understanding of this passive righteousness of faith always result in grave offense to fallen man?

6. Read Genesis 9:20–29. How are we to understand a "righteous man" being so foolish? What do you think could account for the difference in how the sons reacted to their father's indiscretion?

7. A father can teach his children many things. How is teaching them to have faith in God different from teaching them how to manage an ark . . . or their finances?

8. What are some of the best things a man can do to help his children grow to be followers of Christ? What can we learn about this from Noah?

9. Read Genesis 9:1–17. Why is it important that the first Great Commission is reestablished? How does the covenant of the rainbow assert the reality of righteousness before God?

10. In addition to rainbows, what reminders in nature and daily life can help you this week to live as "a righteous man, blameless in his generation" (Genesis 6:9)?

# Abraham

Perhaps you are one of those unfortunate people who have lived long enough in the church to have been endured the singing (with motions, of course, excessively expressive, ridiculously meaningless, hopelessly senseless motions) of the Sunday School and teen youth group classic "Father Abraham." The lyrics are mercifully short:

> Father Abraham had many sons,
> Many sons had Father Abraham.
> I am one of them, and so are you.
> So, let's all praise the Lord!

The words are innocent and perhaps even accurate; with a bit of imagination one might even be able to construe the Gospel within these words. The words are not the problem. The problem is that the one and only verse is repeated ad nauseam, with each successive production of the verse conscripting additional parts of human anatomy in acting (*dancing* is far too dignified a word) the ditty in a manner reminiscent of the "Hokey Pokey."

Still, there *is* something about those words.

It is rightly said that Adam is the father of us all. Not only does the human race find a common origin in our great (raised to the appropriate power) grandfather Adam, but we also share his sin. We are all one in Adam, our corrupt and corrupting father. Abraham has a similar reach in the extent of his fatherhood. Not the father of fallen mankind, Abraham is the father of those who have faith, the father of those who cling to God and the promises of God like Noah did. Indeed, Abraham is the quintessential righteous patriarch—the icon of those who are righteous by faith. The lessons learned in considering Noah apply here as well, as they do in the case of each of the great Old Testament patriarchs. But, there is more that Abraham has to teach us about what it means to be a father who lives with courage. Abraham shows us that fatherhood is very often all about waiting.

Abraham had been a dutiful son, staying by the side of his father, Terah, even when the venerable elder packed up the family and headed west to a strange new land—a land Terah would never see. Abraham did see it, arriving in Canaan when he was seventy-five years old, about the same time that the Lord made a spectacular promise to Abraham (who was technically still just Abram, but that part of the story is not important right now) about his being the father of "a great nation" (Genesis 12:2). That was when the waiting began.

To be the father of a great nation, one needed a son, or at the very least, a child of some kind. And in this regard, Abraham was sorely lacking. Sarah, Abraham's wife, was barren. Abraham's waiting, then, was not like waiting for the fish to bite. It was like waiting for the fish to jump into the boat and clean and fillet themselves.

Abraham waited a full ten years for the incredible promise to come true. But, the waiting got the best of him, and with his Sarah's help he hatched a plan to help God keep His promise (Genesis 16:1–4). After all, God helps those who help themselves, right? Sarah's compliant maid Hagar supplied the womb, and Abraham became the father of Ishmael. Now the plan could move forward. Thirteen years passed before God let Abraham know that He did not need help with the plan. By this time, Abraham had probably become quite comfortable with the way things were moving forward—in spite of the domestic strife between Hagar and the envious Sarah. So, when God reiterated the promise of a great nation, Abraham assumed that it was already in full gear, through Ishmael. The response was unambiguous: "No, but Sarah your wife shall bear you a son, and you shall call his name Isaac" (Genesis 17:19). A year later, the impossible promise was reality.

Just to be unambiguous on another important point: it is not true that God helps those who help themselves. Of course, God does not expect any of His creatures to pray for daily bread and then wait with outstretched hands to catch the manna from on high. But neither does He cooperate with His creatures' honest efforts and reward the industrious ones with special favors. That is a piece of human logic devoid of any scriptural support. In fact, what is clear from the mushrooming mess with Hagar and Ishmael is that when humans get tired of waiting and try to assist God in the execution of His plan, they are notoriously adept at derailing the plan. Ishmael was not the solution, but a serious complication. Abraham needed to learn that his fatherhood would come on God's terms. Which raises a serious question: just how much can a man do when he's waiting for God? If doing nothing can be wrong (as in waiting for bread), how much is too much? The answer is actually quite simple and perfectly illustrated by Abraham. Doing what is humanly possible to accomplish what God has indicated as His plan must always be limited by the will of God. In other words, don't violate a command of God in order to fulfill what you believe is God's will. When Abraham fathered a child with his wife's servant—regardless of the noble motive—he was violating God's intention for marriage (one man and one woman become one flesh for life [Genesis 2:24]). In the ordinary course of life, it is never wise, let alone right, to step outside of God's will in an effort to accomplish God's will. Abraham learned this the hard way.

Well, maybe Abraham was a slow learner. He had his struggles with taking God's Law seriously. On two separate occasions, he introduced Sarah as his sister when he feared another man might decide to make a widow of Sarah in order to rescue her with a new marriage. Apparently in Abraham's world this was a liability of having a beautiful wife (see Genesis 12 and 20). Not surprisingly, at least to everyone but Abraham, it seems, both situations turned ugly. God wants His people to follow Him in obedience. What He says is what they do. But Abraham did learn. And so we come, at last, to the real heart of the Abraham story—the disconcerting, unsettling story of Genesis 22. You know it. "Take your son, your only son Isaac, whom you love, and go to the land of Moriah, and offer him there as a burnt offering" (Genesis 22:2). No ambiguity here. None. And this time, Abraham offers no hesitation, and no attempt to redirect the plan. He gets up early (with anticipation?) packs the beast, takes a couple of servants, some wood, and . . . Isaac . . . and begins the march to Moriah.

Was it a death march, or was it a march of faith? For Abraham, it was both. The agony implicit in waiting a quarter of a century for Isaac's long-deferred arrival is undeniable, but the three-day trip to Moriah for Isaac's premature departure must have eclipsed even that. They went by foot. Each step brought Abraham closer to the horror of fulfilling the command. And then, as Isaac and Abraham make the final ascent alone, we have, at last, the very first biblical dialogue between a father and his son:

> And Isaac said to his father Abraham, "My father!" And he said, "Here am I, my son." He said, "Behold, the fire and the wood, but where is the lamb for a burnt offering?" Abraham said, "God will provide for Himself the lamb for a burnt offering, my son." (Genesis 22:7–8)

The writer to the Hebrews exults in the faith of Abraham revealed in that response (Hebrews 11:17–19). It is not cryptic or evasive. It is the declaration of confidence in a God who will do what needs to be done to accomplish His plan. Abraham will follow the plan—all the way. If it is God's plan to make a great nation of Abraham, and if God is determined to build this nation through Isaac, and if that same God has now commanded the destruction of this promised son, the linchpin of the whole plan, well, then, God will simply have to raise the slaughtered Isaac from the dead!

Abraham had learned to wait. Abraham had learned that the plan belonged to God. Abraham had learned that the long-awaited son belonged to God. Abraham had learned that no human tinkering can force the hand of God, or improve on the plan that God has ordained. This is a lesson that every father must learn. What God has planned, what God has directed, must be fulfilled, even when from a limited human perspective such obedience to the will of God makes no earthly sense.

The fundamental lesson of the story about obedience and trust is easy enough to grasp. A few of the story's details are a bit harder to handle. First, it needs to be understood that this test was not contrived so that God might discover something about His creature. The test was not for the benefit of God, but for the sake of Abraham, and all of us who now hear and ponder this story. God does not need to test us to find out where we stand or to see what we will do in any given situation. Omniscience does not need controlled experiments to gain information. A bigger problem is the composition of this test. There are no simple explanations for the command itself. Why God would demand Abraham to conduct a human sacrifice in the name of worship is not explained in the text and resists a compelling or convincing rationale. Neither is it obvious from the text exactly how Abraham could discern God's specific will in this case when it was such a departure from all that God had previously revealed. What is clear is that we must not take the story as a bizarre biblical license to dispense with what God has revealed about His will through the Law when we want to claim a higher call.

Abraham was accountable to do God's will. So are we. God's will is not variable or self-contradictory. He does not give an individual a secret mission to accomplish that violates His will revealed in Scripture and natural law. This makes the path of obedience a bit easier to negotiate. A man intent on heeding God's will does not walk in mystery and confusion. He follows what has been made plain in God's Word and world. Understood this way, determining God's will is not difficult or confounding. But, of course, this is what makes Abraham's challenge all the more perplexing. Somehow, for some reason, in this unusual situation (the only one in the history of God's dealings with His creation), God directed Abraham to do what was morally unthinkable. No explanation for this exception is entirely satisfying. The inspired author of Hebrews, though, knew better than to allow the ethical dilemma to obscure the profound spiritual truth of this account. The unnamed writer saw clearly that in receiving Isaac back—as far as Abraham was concerned, from death—God was providing a picture of the plan of salvation (Hebrews 11:17–19).

It has been suggested that the central event of God's plan of salvation is itself a horrifying story of divine, cosmic child abuse: the Father sacrificing His innocent, indeed sinless, Son—an event, it is argued, every bit as disturbing and ethically reprehensible as Abraham's own intent to slay Isaac. But, the writer of Hebrews reverses the flow of interpretation. Instead of reading Calvary in the light of Abraham and human judgments of morality and justice, one must read the Genesis story in the light of the fulfillment of Good Friday and Easter. What we see on Mount Moriah is a hint of what will happen in that place centuries later: the Son brutally slaughtered for the sake of the plan. And then, the surprise outcome—suddenly, impossibly—God intervenes and life is the last word after all. No, it is not child abuse. It is the Creator going beyond the limits of human reason or imagination to redeem all of His children. It is the Son so thoroughly trusting His Father that He follows the Father's will all the way—even into and through death and hell itself. It is the Father doing all that is necessary to accomplish the plan—this time with no last-minute substitution of a ram. This time, the Lamb pays the full price and makes the sacrifice. And this time, the resurrection is not figurative; Jesus does not come within a breath of death. This time, He truly, literally dies. And from the depth of death itself, He comes back, gloriously alive. The resurrection is literal and normative.

The resurrection is the literal and normative reality that constitutes the central throbbing core of every Christian believer. Grace is not about a general niceness of God. Faith is not vague trust in some higher power—however you may understand it. No, grace is God's action to rescue His sinful and broken creatures. Grace is God's plan to send the Son, the sacrificial lamb who pays the price and restores the creation. And faith is the redeemed creature's utter trust in God's provision through His Son. This is the essential and nonnegotiable truth of Christianity. This is the thing, above all else, that a father must seek to instill in his children. Whatever a father might teach his child, whether how to tie a shoe, drive a car, treat elders with respect, or keep a promise, nothing matters more than delivering to that child the Gospel message of salvation through the wonderful plan of God accomplished in Jesus. This is the faith that Abraham lived. This is the faith that all Christians share. This is the faith that must animate and motivate the words and actions of every father committed to fulfilling his vocation—his obligation—of fatherhood. Like Abraham, a Christian father recognizes that his child is actually God's child. A faithful father sees with searing clarity the compelling responsibility to raise his children to know their true Father. This requires putting a higher premium on God's Word than on human reason. This requires trusting God through what may be some harrowing times. This requires an acknowledgement that the child and the plan are both God's, and that the father is but the servant striving to honor God's plan and nurture God's child. This requires patient waiting. A Mount Moriah death march might not be part of God's instructions for you, but the course you are given to navigate will certainly make its own demands on your capacity for waiting—and trusting. Doing your fatherhood work the way that God wants it done can be accomplished in no other way.

Thus it is that Abraham is indeed Father Abraham. He is the father of all who live in faith, and of all who strive in that faith to live according to God's plan. "Know then that it is those of faith who are the sons of Abraham" (Galatians 3:7). Genetics and bloodlines are irrelevant. This is a descent of faith. The common bond is not DNA, but Jesus Christ. God did indeed fulfill His promise to Abraham—he fathered a great people and many sons. As the song says, "I am one of them, and so are you." Such knowledge should prompt fitting praise to the Lord and lives lived in conformity with God's will. For a father, there's nothing vague or mysterious about that will. Live in faith, and strive to make sons and daughters of Abraham out of the sons and daughters who call you father.

## Questions

1. Did you sing Sunday School songs? What were your favorites? least favorites?

2. How important are things like the songs sung in Sunday school or VBS for a child's Christian education?

3. Read Genesis 17:1–8, 15–24. Why do you think Abraham was so persistent about God's promise coming through Ishmael even after God had been quite explicit that Sarah would be the mother of the heir? What does this indicate about the character of Abraham?

4. What clues point to the kind of father that Abraham was? What do you think—how far should a father go to loyally defend his child?

5. Turn to Genesis 22 and review the story. Which part of the journey do you believe was most difficult for Abraham? Relate a situation from your own experience when a father had a difficult time following God's will for his child. Why might it be possible that following God's will may actually seem to make very little sense to some people?

6. How does a father, or anyone else, go about determining God's will for specific situations?

7. Why might someone argue that the Father's plan of salvation amounts to cosmic child abuse? How would you respond to such a claim?

8. Referring to Jesus as the Lamb of God (John 1:29) is familiar to most of us. Would there be any value in also calling Him the "Ram of God"?

9. If conversion and preservation of faith are things only God can do (as Luther makes clear in his Small Catechism explanation of the Third Article of the Apostles' Creed), then what role does a father play in transmitting faith to his children?


10. What will you do in the week ahead to live like the son of Abraham that you are?

# Isaac

Parents have been known to saddle their children with some rather unusual and—sometimes unfortunate—names. There are those infants who are encumbered with monstrous names and suffixes presumably meant to evoke images of nobility and prestige. And there are those who are named at the other extreme with hippie names like Rainbow, Moonbeam, or Freedom. There are also those names that can be used, supposedly, for either sex: Leslie, Kim, and Taylor, for example. Young girls probably don't mind answering to one of those versatile names nearly as much as their male counterparts mind it.

But, near the head of the list of unfortunate names must be a Texas woman born in 1882: Ima Hogg. Yes, she actually existed. Her father, James Stephen, was governor of the state. It has often been rumored that Miss Hogg had a sister named Ura, but the truth is Ima had only brothers. Fortunately for Ima, her wealth and philanthropy allowed her to create a legacy that outshone her memorable name.

The Bible certainly contains its share of unusual or difficult names—at least many of them are difficult enough to pronounce—especially in the Old Testament. Still, what a twenty-first-century Western person would consider a challenging name, a Hebrew-speaker would have considered perfectly obvious and normal. But, not all of them. If *Abraham* conveys a sense of dignity and even reverence, then *Isaac* falls at the opposite end of the spectrum. Naturally, this truth is lost on modern English readers of Genesis.

But, those who spoke Hebrew would have marveled at the name given to the son of Abraham and Sarah. It might have raised a few eyebrows. *Isaac* meant, literally, "he laughs." It was a hippie name.

Before we begin to wonder about the character of a father who would foist such a name on a child, we should recall the origin of the name. It was God's idea. Abraham had laughed first. When God told him that Sarah was to be the mother of the promised heir of the covenant, Abraham laughed. From the text, it does not appear to be laughter of joy (Genesis 17:17). Sarah did the same thing when the promise was repeated in her hearing (Genesis 18:12). In spite of the absurdity of it all, the child came, and as God directed, he was named Isaac, "He Laughs." For Abraham and Sarah the laughter was no longer in derision and disbelief, now it was in delicious delight. God had done it. Obediently, they conferred the chosen name.

Just to be clear, Isaac's name was actually a verb. A noun form for laughter was available. But that was not the name. Isaac does not mean laughter. It means "he laughs." Maybe it was a bit awkward for Abraham and Sarah "I'd like you to meet my son, He Laughs." Maybe God intended the odd name to be a perpetual reminder to Abraham, and everyone else who heard the story, not to laugh when God has made a promise. Maybe God was just exercising a healthy sense of humor. Whatever the reason, the name caught on, and children are still named Isaac—now a name with dignity and honor attached.

The anticipation of Isaac's arrival was enormous. With such a buildup, one would legitimately expect this child of promise and divine blessing to accomplish extraordinary things. Surprisingly, though, the biblical stories associated with Isaac are rather tame and ordinary. In fact, the chapters of Genesis that relate the life of Isaac focus more attention on those around him than on Isaac himself. The Mount Moriah incident is Abraham's story. Isaac is a supporting actor at best. Genesis then devotes sixty-seven full verses, an entire chapter, to the search and discovery of the right wife for Isaac. And it is that wife who becomes the central figure in the next big event: the deception of old Isaac and the trickery of Jacob, Isaac's second son.

Isaac doesn't steal many headlines in the scriptural record. Those on either side of him, Abraham and Jacob, get much more attention in Genesis and in the rest of the Bible. There is no record of Isaac sparring with God over the extent of God's mercy toward a condemned city. We don't have any accounts of Isaac leading a small army of men into battle against belligerent kings and raiding parties. There is no dramatic narrative in which God tests the promised heir the way God had tested his father. There are no detailed stories of conniving and intrigue as a young man tries to find security—and then a fortune—in a foreign land living with extended family. Isaac doesn't wrestle all night with the Lord's angel before winning a blessing. Jacob and Abraham are the ones who perform all of these great feats. Isaac has a life that is considerably more quiet and serene. In fact, Isaac's life is utterly uneventful. It is precisely this fact that makes Isaac such a powerful source of insight for ordinary men living in the ordinary routine of ordinary life in an ordinary world.

Perhaps it is not too far a stretch, or reading too much into what is not stated in the text, to draw a connection between Isaac's name and the life he lived. In contrast with the drama and tension that marked the lives of his father and sons, Isaac's own life was tame, leaving him plenty of room to laugh and enjoy it. This is not to imply, much less suggest, that Isaac was indolent or a hedonist striving only to maximize his own pleasure. No, Isaac was a man who had learned well what his father Abraham had taught him, and as a result, he enjoyed the many blessings of a life lived in conformity with God's will.

At age 40, he marries the woman who had been tracked down and won for him by his father's most trusted servant. Together they lived in the rich countryside of southern Canaan. There is a challenge early in the marriage. Rebekah is barren—a terrible curse in a society that counted children as a sure sign of God's particular favor. But, Isaac takes the situation in stride and prays for God to intervene for the sake of his wife. God does. The first set of twins in recorded history is born: Esau and Jacob. Another fifteen years after the birth of the twins, Isaac joins with his brother Ishmael to bury their father, Abraham. It is interesting to consider that the patriarchs interacted not only with their children, but also with their grandchildren. Isaac was living in the warm light of God's favor and practicing what he had learned about a relationship with God founded on humility and trust. The evidence of this is God's specific articulation of a renewed covenant with

Isaac: "Fear not, for I am with you and will bless you and multiply your offspring for My servant Abraham's sake" (Genesis 26:24).

Not everything that Isaac learned from his father was admirable, however. Isaac follows the deceptive and dishonest example of his father point by point when he fears that his wife's beauty will prove a liability and cost him his own life. Famine forced a brief sojourn among the Philistines, so the crafty Isaac emulated his father and introduced his wife as his sister. The ruler of the city caught on to the truth of the matter when he happened to glimpse Isaac in a tender moment with his wife. Interestingly, the word used to describe this intimacy is first translated "to laugh." Secondary translations are to amuse oneself or to play with or even playfully touch another. Isaac was enjoying his wife!

Once Isaac's game of deception was exposed, he lived a charmed life among the Philistines. In fact, "The LORD blessed him, and the man became rich, and gained more and more until he became very wealthy" (Genesis 26:12–13). It is not an endorsement of prosperity-Gospel ideas to acknowledge that Isaac's success and blessing were products of the choices he made. In other words, Isaac's life of faith and piety provided the setting within which Isaac prospered. It's not automatic, but there is an undeniable correlation between the choices a person makes and the sort of life he experiences. The result of Isaac's remarkable affluence was altogether predictable: "The Philistines envied him" (Genesis 26:14). Of course they did.

It is always the same. When God's blessings are flowing in the life of a man, and when that man has the audacity to revel in the goodness God is giving, people around are not inclined to celebrate with him. They are, in fact, prone to resent his good gifts, begrudge his happiness, and envy his prosperity. Things have changed little in four thousand years; more accurately, *people* have changed little in four thousand years. This experience is not uncommon even within God's Church; even there, people are still people, and envy is still a problem. Given the reality of man's sinful nature, and the consistency with which he demonstrates that nature, it should not shock us when envy works with its poison to destroy the peace and blessing God gives. It shouldn't shock, but it does disappoint. Envy is a sore affliction among God's people, causing untold grief. It is a sad fact that even Christians are often more ready to disparage the man who is enjoying the blessing of God than they are ready to celebrate with him. And it is a sad fact that those who should be multiplying our joy often seek to diminish it instead. Isaac knew these truths intimately. Fallen creatures that we are, we often find it difficult to laugh with those who laugh.

It was envy, or at least a heavy dose of sibling rivalry (is there a difference?), that motivated what is one of the most memorable (and perhaps most painful) moments in the record of Isaac. It is precisely this same event that relates one of the few direct interactions between Isaac and his twin sons. Of course, the event is the Sunday School standard, the "stealing of the blessing."

This story is as much Jacob's story as it is part of Isaac's history. But, it does give some insight into Isaac and his role of father. We know next to nothing about what life was like in the family tents of Abraham and Isaac. But, we know that when Isaac decided it was time to give to his firstborn, Esau, the blessing that was rightly his, Rebekah decided it was time for her to act and make sure that God's Word (Genesis 25:23) was fulfilled for the sake of Jacob.

It might be tempting to read into this story a failure on the part of Isaac to resolve what seems to have been a simmering tension between his twin sons. But the text does not allow us to draw such conclusions. Neither can we assert any sort of favoritism on the part of Isaac. Giving the blessing of the firstborn to Esau was Isaac's responsibility. He was fulfilling his task as father. That wife and son conspired to deceive Isaac is appalling—not shocking (given fallen man's capacity for endlessly inventive avenues of sin, nothing that man does should shock), but certainly appalling. Isaac, and we, should expect better of Rebekah and Jacob. But the deed is done. Regardless of the motives, Isaac is mocked. Mother and son do not laugh with the patriarch, but at him.

Isaac was resilient, however. He would laugh again, in delight at the blessing of God. The Genesis record tells us nothing about discussions and restoration subsequent to the crisis of family deception. But, something of the sort must have occurred to allow Isaac to extend a blessing and admonition to his second-born when it became necessary for Jacob to leave the tents of home. Fratricide was in the air. Discretion was in order. Jacob would go to Rebekah's brother Laban. Before he departed for the distant land, however, the deceiver was summoned to Isaac. This time, he went without deception or pretense; this time, Isaac gave his blessings freely. Isaac had resigned himself to the *fait accompli*. He blessed the younger son with the blessing that belonged to the covenant heir. The promise given to Abraham and renewed for Isaac would be fulfilled through the line of Jacob—the one who would be Israel. Even through and in spite of man's sinful actions, God's plan is advanced. The plan will not be thwarted. So, Isaac blessed his son with the blessing of Abraham (Genesis 28:3–4), and Isaac admonished his son with a directive of his own.

The paternal admonition that Jacob received contains a valuable lesson, indeed even an exhortation, for fathers of every time and place. The patriarch had been deceived, but he was still sharp about what mattered. And what mattered was that Jacob be given every advantage for the task before him. He was the heir of the promise, the one to communicate God's truth to the next generation. God's plan would unfold through him. Not surprisingly, then, Isaac was exceedingly concerned about a wife for Jacob. No doubt, the memory of Abraham's enormous investment in securing his own wife from what was presumably virtuous family stock helped to prompt a similar concern for the selection of a bride for Jacob. Esau's choices—Canaanite women—brought grief to his parents (Genesis 26:34–35). Jacob would need to make a much better choice. Isaac was explicit: "You must not take a wife from the Canaanite women" (Genesis 28:1). Following Abraham's example, Isaac had a better plan. Jacob should find a fitting bride in the household of Uncle Laban (Genesis 28:1–3).

Obviously, Isaac knew something about family dynamics and the powerful influence a wife has on the thinking and acting of her husband. He knew that the heir of God's promise needed to be supported by a wife who would also treasure God's covenant promise. Jacob's helpmate needed to be a true help to him, not a woman who might not share his commitment to his heritage. There was a grave risk that a foreign wife would not hold the promises of Yahweh with sufficient regard. Isaac would not risk the chance of Jacob being led to cheapen or discount the tremendous privilege and responsibility he had as the covenant-bearing heir. Isaac considered a Canaanite wife a liability for his chosen son, and he did not hesitate to intervene in the affairs of his son to ensure that the right wife was found.

The thought that a twenty-first-century Christian father should have similar concern for a son's choice of a mate probably seems right. Much harder to imagine is the same father actually giving specific and explicit direction to his son about his dating and marrying choices. The entrenched and endemic cultural doctrines, (actually, heresies) about the sovereignty of the individual, personal autonomy, self-realization, and free will all conspire to cripple a father when it comes to helping his son precisely when he needs it most—when he is choosing a partner for the rest of his life. Few decisions have more profound significance on a man's life, yet too many Christian fathers appear unable or unwilling to actively help a son choose well. Isaac offers a challenging counterexample.

In many ways on many levels, Isaac, the ordinary, nothing special patriarch, has much to teach us. Without the benefit of gripping tales of testing or valiant vignettes of conquest and triumph, Isaac still manages to provide a remarkable portrait of a courageous father. In the face of opposition and conflict fueled by envy, he lived his life the way God had called him to live it. When his son needed direction, he did not hesitate to give it. On one level, Isaac's life was altogether ordinary. On another level, it was altogether remarkable. Sometimes courageous living is as simple—and as demanding—as living with consistent obedience and parenting with persistent presence and guidance. The man with the memorable name lived with such courage and so had good reason to laugh. So, too, did his father—and his God. The plan was continuing to unfold.


## Questions

1. What are some of the more memorable names you can recall? What significance does your name have?

2. Scripture relates two crucial, formative events in the life of Isaac. What impact do you think the event at Mount Moriah had on Isaac (Genesis 22)? What about the successful mission to find a wife for him (Genesis 24)?

3. What are some formative moments in your life that have left a mark that remains to this day?

4. Read Genesis 26:6–22, where Isaac contends with the envious Philistines. What is odd or surprising about the story? What does Isaac's response tell us about his character?

5. What fatherhood lesson might be derived from Isaac's handling of the well incident (Genesis 26:17–22)? How would this make a difference for the fathers you know?

6. Does the "stealing of the blessing" (Genesis 27:26–45) indicate a dysfunctional family with significant problems? What other interpretations might there be of this text? How can God's blessing to Isaac be at work in this situation?

7. In Old Testament passages that invoke the patriarchs, Isaac is sandwiched between his father and son (for example, see Deuteronomy 30:20). What does Isaac's role as link (Genesis 26:4) between Father Abraham and the man who will be Israel teach us about our roles within God's plan?

8. Read Genesis 27:41–28:5. Who had the idea of Jacob finding a wife in the tents of Laban? What role do you think parents today should have in a child's choice of a spouse?

9. Jacob's "a while" (Genesis 27:44) with Laban turned into twenty years. We are never told whether Rebekah saw her son again, but Isaac did. Read Genesis 35:27–29. What significance would this meeting have had for Isaac?

10. The pronoun in Isaac's name is wonderfully ambiguous. Abraham and Sarah laughed. What about Rebekah, Jacob, and Isaac himself? What about God? In what sense could each of these have been the ones who laughed?

# Jacob

*Way, way back many centuries ago,*
*Not long after the Bible began,*
*Jacob lived in the land of Canaan,*
*A fine example of a family man.*

Thus, we are introduced to Jacob by Tim Rice, and it's not a bad introduction at that. Regardless of one's further assessment of *Joseph and the Amazing Technicolor Dreamcoat*, at least here the musical offers a fair—and even flattering—representation of the patriarch. To be remembered as a great family man is a legacy of which any man, including Jacob, could be proud. And Jacob certainly fits the description. The husband of two wives and the father of twelve sons (and at least two daughters [Genesis 37:35]), Jacob knew something about heading up a family. He was a family man, no doubt. Given the size and complexities of his family, it's probably a fair assumption that he possessed a good deal of courage. Merely shouldering the burden of providing for such a family would have demanded a healthy dose of courage, but considering the sort of issues that came to define Jacob's expansive family, courage was a necessity. So, Jacob, the fine example of a family man, should provide some practical and pointed lessons for the fathers of later generations—including ours.

It will not, however, be quite that simple. In fact, the length of Jacob's life and the relentless flood of trouble that he endured make a glowing, rosy assessment of Jacob's life more difficult, if not impossible. Jacob thought the same, telling Pharaoh that the years of his life (130 at that point) had been "few and evil" (Genesis 47:9). Maybe it was merely a bit of self-effacement, or perhaps Jacob was evaluating his own life in the light of his father Isaac's rather charmed life, or most likely, it was simply the truth. Jacob lived a life filled with dramatic contrasts. In addition to his dozen sons—a sign of great blessing in his world—Jacob also had enormous wealth (Genesis 30:43) and the favor of God (Genesis 28:15). But, none of these things came to him easily. His dozen sons came in the midst of trickery (on the part of father-in-law, Laban) and rivalry (on the part of the sisters-become-wives, Leah and Rachel). His wealth was won through twenty years of hard work and animosity between him and Laban. And the blessing of God seemed always to be tied to intense competition, wrestling, and struggle—sometimes literally (Genesis 32:24). Nothing was ever neat and clean or by the book for Jacob. The people who surrounded him certainly made life difficult. Yet, it was probably Jacob himself who inflicted the greatest sorrow, woe, and heartache on Jacob. He is a complicated character.

Holy Scripture records a wealth of detail about the life of Jacob, providing more material than a short study can even begin to consider. Through the long, meandering narrative, though, common themes begin to emerge. In fact, two words seem to capture the tumultuous life of Jacob: *deception* and *blessing*. One word is sinister and ugly; the other is delightful and warm. One word is born in the world of darkness and evil; the other originates always in the goodness of God. A greater contrast is difficult to imagine. But, deception and blessing are the story of Jacob. In his story, the antithetical poles are brought together, and God's plan is advanced again.

From the moment of his birth, there was *something* about Jacob. His twin, Esau, beat him into the world, but Jacob was hard on the heels of the firstborn—actually grasping the heel of his big brother. Hence his name: "one who takes by the heel or supplants" (see Genesis 25:26). *Heel-grabber*: it has an ominous ring about it. A heel-grabber is the guy who's always playing catch-up but managing, somehow, to pull some measure of success out of his awkward or compromised position. The heel-grabber is the quarterback who makes a desperate lunge at the seven-yard line and just clips the heel of the lineman—the one who miraculously had found a deflected pass in his tree-trunk arms and started lumbering toward the goal line only to crash headlong in an awful heap of flesh and equipment, just short of the end zone, just short of the full glory. The heel-grabber is the spoiler who tarnishes the dream and soils the happiness of others. The heel-grabber makes a career of it. Jacob was a heel-grabber. He connived. He deceived. He cheated. There's plenty about Jacob not to like.

Jacob consistently confirmed the legitimacy of his name. He took advantage of Esau (a man saddled with his own set of problems and issues—the most glaring, a dullness that too often crippled his discernment) and traded a meal for Esau's birthright (Genesis 25:29–34). With the help of his mother (was he perhaps a bit of a momma's boy? [Genesis 25:27–29]), Jacob maneuvered through an elaborate scheme and tricked Isaac into giving him the blessing of the firstborn—Esau's blessing. Maybe, Jacob had merely perfected the tired habits of his father and grandfather. Remember, both Abraham and Isaac had demonstrated some degree of moral handicap when it came to telling the truth about a beautiful wife. But, Jacob's deception goes well beyond what his forebears had found acceptable. Blatantly self-serving and covetous, Jacob's deception has a particularly foul stench about it. Jacob's heel-grabbing nature continued with his willingness to embrace a desperate woman's plan and father children through a servant, and then another four times (Genesis 30:1–13).

And even as a father, Jacob famously cheated his ten oldest sons, loving Rachel's long-awaited firstborn, Joseph, more than any of the rest and making no effort to conceal his preference (Genesis 37:3–4). Jacob's folly was made tangible in the notorious "coat of many colors," and the brothers' treacherous treatment of Jacob's favorite may have been dismaying, but it was hardly surprising.

Jacob was not exaggerating when he described his life as hard. But, it seems that Jacob's greatest woes were ultimately self-inflicted. After all, what goes around comes around. The one who was prone to underhanded acts and devious dealing was often the victim of reciprocal trickery from others—maybe Jacob proved an inspiration to them. Jacob's dear uncle Laban ruined his nephew's wedding day with the ultimate bait and switch: on the first morning of Jacob's honeymoon, it was Leah, with "weak eyes," who was sharing his marriage bed, and not Rachel, the sister who was easy on the eyes, the one for whom he had labored seven years

(Genesis 29:21–26). Though the details are less than clear to modern readers, it is clear enough that Laban's shady practices continued when it came to the family business of sheep-ranching and Jacob's compensation (Genesis 30:25–43 and 31:38–42).

And it was his own sons who brought the greatest tragedy and comfortless grief to the aging Jacob when they fooled their father by shredding that despised multi-colored coat and adding one more color to the mix—goat's-blood red. Jacob could not get over the loss of his favorite son. Even in death, Joseph was still the favorite, and the strife in the family churned unabated. For all the privilege and wealth that surrounded Jacob, his life was not easy. He paid a hefty price for his crooked habits and his dishonest practices.

To his credit, though, Jacob was not one to allow a difficult situation to cripple or define him. Indeed, it was often his unfortunate circumstances that prompted his most resourceful and courageous actions. In the end, he got the better of his unscrupulous uncle and returned to Canaan leading a caravan of unrivaled prosperity. Jacob was even able to reconcile with his brother, Esau, by executing a careful plan of appeasement (Genesis 32–33). The bare description of that final climactic fraternal confrontation is a delightful instance of the scriptural narrative's capacity for profound emotional impact and sublime beauty (Genesis 33:4). Esau running to embrace his brother is a potent image. So is the mental picture that is painted when the text later tells us that when Isaac reached the end of his days, it was his twin sons who together buried him with his fathers. It is comforting and hopeful to see Esau and Jacob reconciled. And, when Jacob reaches his own end, we are again given a picture of reconciliation and tenderness: against all odds, the wound that could not be healed, the loss of Joseph, has been healed after all. Repentance, forgiveness, harmony, and hope mark the last days of Jacob. Confident of God's promise, he blesses all of his sons before he dies. Deceit and blessing and the courage to cling to the covenant promise—this is the story of Jacob. It is an important and encouraging lesson. Even if the pain, challenge, and sorrow of life are self-created, the result of your *own* sinful choices and actions, the struggle to live courageously, tenaciously, and faithfully can bring surprising blessing. The lesson seems obvious—but it's not right, at least not entirely.

Blessing in spite of deceitfulness raises a significant problem. Particularly in light of Psalm 24, it raises a significant challenge to the neat, logical lesson we'd like to derive from Jacob's life. Inspired by the Spirit, David makes a sweeping assertion that should make us all stop a moment and wonder about exactly how God's plan hangs together.

> Who shall ascend the hill of the LORD?
> And who shall stand in His holy place?
> He who has clean hands and a pure heart,
> who does not lift up his soul to what is false
> and does not swear deceitfully.
> He will receive blessing from the LORD
> and righteousness from the God of his salvation.
> Psalm 24:3–5

The standard established here seems to leave little room for a man like Jacob. One could parse words and quibble about whether Jacob actually *swore* deceitfully or *lifted up his soul* to lies and falsehood—whatever concrete meaning that phrase may carry. But facts are hard things to ignore, and the scriptural record itself calls Jacob's actions deceitful (Genesis 27:35; 31:20). Jacob fits the bill: he was a deceiver, and therefore excluded from the presence of God—or so it would seem. But then David completes his thought:

> Such is the generation of those who seek Him,
> who seek the face of the God of Jacob.
> Psalm 24:6

Obviously, David does not consider Jacob to be in view when he rails against liars and deceivers. Apparently, neither does God, who blesses Jacob again and again and again (Genesis 28:13–15; 31:3; 32:24–30; 35:9–12; 46:2–4). In fact, God extends to Jacob the greatest blessing of all, choosing him to be the critical generation— it was all of his sons who were to be the forebears of the tribes of Israel. From his deathbed in Goshen, Jacob proved to be a master at blessing. Every one of the twelve sons was blessed (Genesis 49). Not one was overlooked. No more singling out one son to be the heir of the promise. Now, all would inherit the promise. Now, all of Israel's sons would be God's people. Yes, these chosen people were the sons of Abraham, but the name that defined them was *children of Israel*. Those twelve sons of Jacob were the ones who would give their names to their descendants forever: Moses would be from Levi, Saul from Benjamin, David from Judah. Every man knew his heritage. Descended from one of Jacob's twelve sons, he was a son of Israel.

Israel—the beautiful, blessed name—has appeared at last. But, how can this be? How can the supplanter, the deceiver, the heel-grabber escape the curse of God and receive instead the blessing of God? How can Jacob become Israel? It is tempting to offer some solution, some explanation that will make the choice of Jacob palatable, or at least reasonable. There must be some justification for God's persistent determination to bless Jacob in spite of his less than exemplary character and actions. There must be something that Jacob does or will do to disperse the cloud of mystery obscuring and confusing the logic of God's unfolding covenant plan. St. Paul disagrees. God's apostle is not interested in explanations; he's interested in grace. To find some reasonable explanation, Paul knew, would mean speculating beyond what Scripture actually records. Even worse, to offer some reason for God's choice to bless actually destroys the wonder and comfort of sheer grace. This is Paul's point in Romans 9. Christians tend to avoid the hard argument of the apostle in the midst of his Letter to the Romans, but Paul is merely stating what the reader of Genesis knows already. God blesses simply because He chooses to bless. There is no other reason.

> And not only so, but also when Rebekah had conceived children by one man, our forefather Isaac, though they were not yet born and had done nothing either good or bad—in order that God's purpose of election might continue, not because of works but because of Him who calls—she was told, "The older will serve the younger." As it is written, "Jacob I loved, but Esau I hated."
>
> Romans 9:10–13

God offers no explanation, no rationale, no justification. God just makes the choice. Grace is simply delivered. Not because of Jacob, but in spite of Jacob, the blessing is given—the plan of redemption and restoration is advanced. It wasn't Jacob's courage that made it happen. It wasn't his tenacity that earned God's favor. It wasn't his cunning or clever resourcefulness that brought the blessing. God blessed because God had decided to bless.

Deception and blessing are at work side by side and even hand in hand in the story of Jacob—and nowhere more than in the renaming of the patriarch. It is a savory slice of irony that Jacob, who makes a career of being the heel-grabbing supplanter, is himself finally and completely out-maneuvered by God. Right in the middle of Jacob's greatest gambit—his escape from Laban and reconciliation with Esau—just when the cunning and courage of Jacob is being confirmed in a stunning success, God comes to Jacob and supplants him. The struggle is tangible—the famous all-night wrestling match (Genesis 32:24–32).

The text might seem to indicate that it was a close contest, and that by demanding a blessing as the day broke, Jacob controlled the outcome. But, one must remember that God is never wrestled to a draw. It takes only a touch from his opponent, and Jacob's thigh is dislocated. The entire wrestling match unfolded exactly as God intended. The outcome was God's design. Jacob is overcome. Jacob is replaced with Israel. Jacob walks away from his struggle with a limp—much more than that, he walks away a different man. Jacob is gone—the heel-grabber has himself been supplanted, beaten by God, destroyed by God. Israel has been born. That this was entirely the doing of God is clear a couple of chapters later, when God confirms the name change:

> Your name is Jacob; no longer shall your name be called Jacob, but Israel shall be your name.
>
> Genesis 35:10

God is directing the process. It is His plan. God blesses because He chooses to bless. Jacob is God's man because God chooses him. Another father is used to accomplish God's purpose.

The blessing is not man's to earn, but God's to give. And blessed is the man who learns, as Jacob learned, to live at peace within God's plan, yielding to the design of the Creator who accomplishes His purposes through His people. Whether life is short or long, easy or hard, is not the point. Isaac had it easy; Jacob had it hard. Both were used by God. What matters is God's purpose, what matters is what God accomplishes through His man. And what God accomplishes is the making of a people for His own. What God accomplishes is the delivery of grace.

# Questions

1. Big families are not as common today as they once were. What do you know about big families? What might be the advantages and disadvantages of being part of a big family?

2. Western culture has begun to look at large families with curiosity or even suspicion. Why do you think this is so? What things should Christians take into account when thinking about the right size for a family?

3. It is often argued that particular sins are generational, passing from father to son. What do you think of this idea? Does the story of Jacob confirm or refute the idea? How does one overcome "family sins"?

4. Read Genesis 27:18–29, 35. How bad is Jacob's deception? What is he willing to do to accomplish his trick? How would you expect God to respond to Jacob's subterfuge?

5. What does Jacob hear when God confronts him as he flees from Esau? Read Genesis 28:10–17. How do you account for this?

6. Genesis chapter 30 records the tumultuous relationship between the sisters Leah and Rachel. Read verses 1–24. What role does Jacob play? What about this is God pleasing?

7. Read Genesis 32:24–32. In your opinion, what is most significant in this account? Jacob's new name means "one who strives with God." How fitting is this name? Does this name still accurately apply to God's new Israel, the Church?

8. How important is it for a parent to show impartiality toward his children? How is this done when children are obviously quite different from one another? Why do you think Jacob was apparently oblivious to this basic parenting axiom?

9. How does the complexity of Jacob's life and character illuminate Paul's evaluation in Romans 9:10–13? Why is Paul's definitive argument essential for a right understanding of grace?

10. When all is said and done, what do you think about Jacob? What lessons does he teach you?

# David

David needs no introduction. Almost everyone has heard the name—one of the most familiar and still common of any ancient name. The humble shepherd who does the impossible, Israel's greatest king, the first of a dynasty promised to last for eternity: such is David. Even someone who has never read the Bible knows something about David. He may never have cracked a Bible; nevertheless, the most irreligious man is familiar with that millennia-old metaphor that has such remarkable persistence in the world of sports and politics. One well-aimed shot from a sling, and the little guy can bring down a giant. David is the unlikely hero: the underdog who defies all the odds and comes out on top. Everyone loves a David and Goliath story and outcome—well, everyone except Goliath and his fan base.

David's triumph over the arrogant and blasphemous giant is more than enough to immortalize the man and his legend. But, David's success with his sling is only the first entry on what became an impressive résumé of accomplishments. More than eight hundred years elapsed between the time Jacob's sons buried their father (and so laid to rest the age of the patriarchs) and the beginning of David's story. Israel's bondage in Egypt, the exodus, the conquest of Canaan, and the period of the judges is all history for David. But now, David is going to add his own pages to that history and advance Israel's story in ways that his forefathers would have thought impossible apart from their tenacious faith in

God's promise. David brings the golden age of Israel—but not immediately.

After felling Goliath and checking, for a time, the threat of the Philistines (1 Samuel 17), David joins the royal household of Saul, and waits. God has rejected Saul as king, and the shepherd-become-hero has already been anointed as king to succeed Israel's first, failed king (1 Samuel 16). There remains, however, one small obstacle for David—Saul is still alive and still king. Another man would have been tempted to take matters into his own hands and give a little push to God's plan. Abraham and Jacob had both done as much. But David will not. In fact, one of the singular accomplishments of David is his flat refusal to take any action against Saul—even when that means false accusations against his character, loss of his wife, and a difficult life on the run for years. During those long years, twice Saul had wandered unwittingly into the midst of David's concealed men, and twice David had rejected the providential opportunity and allowed Saul safely to depart (1 Samuel 24; 26). His motive was simple: Saul was God's chosen king, and until God removed him from the throne, Saul was David's king. When Saul was vindictive and malicious, David was loyal and submissive. No matter what, David trusted God's promise and waited. David's patient restraint and unwavering faith in God's plan are arguably his greatest accomplishments. But there is much more.

A full account is impractical, but it is worth noting a few more of those admirable accomplishments. Loyalty was a standout trait of David, demonstrated not only in his dealing with Saul, but also in his interactions with Saul's heir, Jonathan (1 Samuel 20). A generation later, David remembered and kept his promise to Jonathan (2 Samuel 9). When at last Saul dies in battle, David does not rejoice. Rather, he grieves the fallen king (2 Samuel 1).

Of course, David also possessed a good portion of more ordinary kingly qualities. He demonstrated unrivaled military prowess, uniting the twelve tribes of Israel under his leadership, finally subduing the Philistines, and conquering Jerusalem as the royal seat of Israel's kingdom (2 Samuel 5). Even what may have been David's darkest deed provided another glimpse into the virtuous character of the man. Of course, there was nothing virtuous about David's sin with Bathsheba and his subsequent crimes perpetrated in an effort to cover up his lustful misdeed

(2 Samuel 11). David was utterly human and utterly sinful. Like every man, he was capable of appalling evil—a fact that should make every man stop and consider the weakness and wickedness of his own flesh. Yet, this infamous episode in David's life eventuates in David's unconditional repentance. Unlike his predecessor, unlike so many sinners caught in the act, David did not protest the charge, shunt the accusations aside, offer excuses, or dodge the guilt. He collapsed in unadorned confession, saying, "I have sinned against the LORD" (2 Samuel 12:13). This willingness to admit his evil action and accept responsibility for the consequences—even very painful and harsh consequences—is a mark of the man's character. It was not the sin of the man, but the humility of the man in evidence when confronted with his sin, for which God called him "a man after My heart" (Acts 13:22). On many levels, David was a singular individual who demonstrated exemplary character, leadership, courage, and piety.

One could gain a treasure of positive lessons from a careful study of David and his efforts to follow God and God's plan. Much of what David has to teach is obvious: patience, humility, tenacity, faith, and, yes, courage, are all wonderfully exemplified in the life of David. These aspects of David's life are familiar; wise and blessed is the man who not only considers them, but who emulates them. From the perspective of our emphasis on fatherhood, however, one of the more important lessons to be learned from David does not lie on the surface. A careful and critical reading of David's story yields a vitally important warning for any father—any parent—striving to live faithfully.

Before that exploration begins, though, it should be noted that finding negative lessons in the life of a patriarch of faith is not an effort to disparage the legacy of the man or the veracity of his life. It is not revisionist history to acknowledge the struggles, mistakes, and even abject failures of great men in the history of the Bible and the Church. The Bible itself makes no attempt to sugarcoat the stories of the saints of old. A patriarch, a pillar of faith, is still a man: a sinner by birth and action, and a saint by faith and forgiveness. This was the case for Adam, Noah, Abraham, Isaac, and Jacob. It is the case for every man—including every hero of the faith. David is no exception. David's ridiculous, horrendous, adulterous crime against Bathsheba, Uriah, his own family, his own nation, and God, is so familiar that it has become part of the lexicon of the Western world. The repercussions of that sin gained incalculably greater force and momentum, however, by another less-recognized but equally destructive sin.

Sins of commission are easy to spot. Sins of omission are not so apparent, and usually fuel much debate over exactly what constitutes sin. To slash some guy's tires out of spite is a sin. To drive by a guy who could use help fixing a flat along a country road—that may or may not be a sin. It's a matter of interpretation. It depends on a host of possible extenuating circumstances, mitigating factors, personal issues, and . . . you get the idea.

Few would dispute the sinfulness of David's lustful actions against Bathsheba and company. But many will disagree or at least remain unsure about the sinfulness of David's sin of omission. Whether a sin of commission or omission, though, sin remains sin and the consequences of either can be equally devastating. David's great sin of omission was not unrelated to his great sin of commission. David's sin: failure in his role as father. Yes, it is a serious charge; such an accusation demands proof.

Actually, David's failure in his role as father can be seen as one aspect of a broader failure to fulfill his responsibilities toward his own family. The case will be made that among David's greatest failures was his domestic failure. He dropped the ball at home. While the familial problems of David eventually snowballed into an enormous nation-engulfing disaster, it may well be that the problems all began with David's basic problem with women. It hardly seems unduly harsh or unfair to suggest that David had difficulty saying no to women. We've already mentioned Bathsheba. Nothing more needs to be discussed on that topic. But there's more. David married Saul's daughter Michal (1 Samuel 18). And then he married Abigail (1 Samuel 25:43). And then he married Ahinoam (1 Samuel 25:42). And then he married Maacah, Hagith, Abital, and Eglah. He wasn't done. "And David took more concubines and wives from Jerusalem, after he came from Hebron, and more sons and daughters were born to David" (2 Samuel 5:13).

David had been blessed with six sons from wives two through seven. His Jerusalem conquests netted him eleven more. Of course, one could interpret such "romantic success" and fertility as marks of the blessing of God. But that's an incorrect interpretation because God had anticipated and precluded this royal temptation:

"He [a king] shall not acquire many wives for himself" (Deuteronomy 17:17). David did not obey—or maybe he simply had a more relaxed definition of "acquire many." Regardless of his motive, the result of David's domestic decisions was disaster.

One incident is especially illustrative of the domestic chaos in the David's court. David's firstborn, Amnon—the heir apparent—made the mistake of falling in love (Amnon's description, though wonders if he knew love from lust) with his half-sister Tamar. The story gets complicated, but the bottom line is that after manipulating the assistance of his unwitting father, Amnon raped Tamar and then rejected her. Tamar's brother, Absalom, came to the aid of his sister and took the unfortunate woman into his own house.

So what does David do about this vile, disgraceful crime among his own children? It is the right question. He is the father (and king) of everyone involved. This is David's mess to fix. This time the text satisfies our curiosity: "When King David heard of all these things, he was very angry" (2 Samuel 13:21). That's it. Don't wait for anything more. There isn't anything more. David did nothing. He got "very angry" and did nothing. His own son commits a perverse and devastating crime against his own daughter, and the best David can muster in response is anger. The father takes no action, neither for justice nor for compassion.

Absalom, on the other hand, is not inactive. He cares for Tamar, taking justice into his own hands. Hatching his own elaborate plot, complete with the king's unwitting complicity, Absalom plays vigilante, and avenges his sister. He kills Amnon.

So, what did David do after this dramatic, bloody development? "David mourned for his son day after day" (2 Samuel 13:37). Absalom, meanwhile, saw the wisdom of departing Israel and went into a three-year, self-imposed exile, languishing in the court of his maternal grandfather, the king of Geshur. For his part, David "longed to go out to Absalom, because he was comforted about Amnon, since he was dead" (2 Samuel 13:39). David, the man of action, proves to be a father of inaction. As the story continues to unfold, David remains consistent, unable or unwilling to act when his own family is concerned.

Did David's paternal inaction amount to sin? It is easy to offer a list of compelling reasons to excuse David's behavior: his children were adults and they were responsible for themselves, David hoped to guide his children by love, not punishment, David was preoccupied with the affairs of state, blended families face special challenges, and so forth.

But the real issue is simply this: Did David fulfill his vocation as father? The answer is obvious. David failed. And when David refused to act and fulfill his task, others were left to fend for themselves and attempt what David should have done. Chaos and heartache inevitably followed. After confronting David for his wickedness in the sin against Bathsheba, Nathan the prophet had continued with a chilling announcement: "The sword shall never depart from your house" (2 Samuel 12:10). This may have been a reference to the nation's state of affairs, a prediction of lingering warfare with no peace for king or people. But Nathan was not finished. The consequences of David's sin would hit close to home: "Thus says the LORD, 'Behold, I will raise up evil against you out of your own house'" (2 Samuel 12:11).

Maybe that was it. Maybe Nathan's prediction accounts for David's inaction. When evil appeared in his own family, David realized he could do nothing about it since it was God's will and resigned himself to "taking his medicine." The medicine was bitterer than he could have guessed. Absalom's alienation resulted in full-blown rebellion and civil war (2 Samuel 15–18). David was disgraced. Regardless of Nathan's prediction, however, David was still responsible. Inaction was sin.

Inaction, like discretion, may sometimes be the better part of valor and the wise course. But inaction may as easily be sin. When a father fails to instruct, guide, protect, and encourage his children, he is failing to do what God has given him to do. He is sinning. There are no mitigating circumstances that justify or minimize such sin. In fact, the reality is that a sin against one's own children will often metastasize with alarming fury and yield inconceivable consequences. How could David have guessed that his failure to take action against Amnon would nurture the increase of a chain of evil that would end in civil war?

David's legendary success as Israel's greatest king does not minimize his family sin. David's great character, humble spirit, and willingness to receive correction do not excuse his family failure. David's profound poetry and sublime songs of prayer and praise— a full third of the Psalms—do not compensate for his domestic desertion. David's sincere piety and genuine faith in God—a man after God's own heart—do not justify his sin against his children. This is hard to grasp, perhaps, but true nonetheless. A man's right standing before God, by grace through faith, does not free him of his responsibilities toward those around him. He may be saved, but he must still serve. Neither does a man's success in one venue absolve him of failure in another. Finally, the sovereign purposes of God and even the punishments of God are never an excuse for compounding guilt by failing to do what needs to be done. Divine sovereignty does not negate human responsibility. No matter why it had happened, David needed to take action against Amnon—to say nothing of what David should have been doing to recognize and prevent such evil before it ever came to its fruition.

These are difficult and uncomfortable lessons to be learned from the life of a great man of God. There is no joy in this investigation. It would be so much more pleasant simply to focus on the good qualities of David and find inspiration in his example. It would be comforting just to contemplate the lessons about repentance and forgiveness that emerge from the Bathsheba ordeal. And it would be nice if today every successful man always fulfilled his responsibilities toward his family.

The mistake, the sin, of David is still viable and deadly in our world. It remains a serious temptation. Men who are busy with important work, busy helping others, busy making contributions to the good of the world, must be careful not to fall into David's great sin of omission and neglect their responsibility toward their own family. We know that it happens. Wonderful men who do wonderful things, too often do a woeful job of being fathers. There is no excuse. The world, and even the Church, might be reluctant to look past a successful man's public accomplishments to consider the health and legacy of that man's family, but God holds the man accountable for what matters. Fatherhood is a sacred responsibility. Fatherhood failure is sin. The consequences of that sin are devastating. We learn that from David. We learn that from our own lives. And so we delight all the more in the greatest lesson to be learned from David: no matter what the sin, God's grace in Christ abounds. No human failure can trump that grace. No man's sin can overcome that love.

# Questions

1. What's your favorite story from the life of David? What is it about this story that holds the attraction for you?

2. What would you consider to be the greatest achievement in the life of David? How does this achievement contribute to your understanding of David's character?

3. How do David's personal accomplishments correlate with his standing before God? Why would God consider David to be a man after His own heart?

4. Read 2 Samuel 11:1–5. What clues about David's character might be revealed in these verses?

5. Read 2 Samuel 13:1–29. What parts of this sad account particularly catch your attention? Discuss the actions and character of each of the individuals involved. What influence might David's own experience in the previous two chapters have had on his response in this situation?

6. What do you think about David's response to the sin of Amnon? Make a case for why you think David's action was or was not sinful. What makes it so much harder to pin down sins of omission, even in our own lives?

7. Is it fair to accuse David of domestic failure in spite of his otherwise remarkably successful and exemplary life? Can you give some recent examples of this same failure evident in the homes of otherwise successful men? Why might we be reluctant to admit this phenomenon?

8. Fathers busy with work that is important in the world and in the church might be tempted to give that work more weight than their work at home with children. What advice do you think David would have if he was included in a discussion on this topic? When it comes to raising children, is quality time more important than quantity time?

9. Read Matthew 22:41–46. What is the relationship between David and Jesus? How should this affect your view of David?

10. Think about John Bradford's famous quote "There, but by the grace of God, go I." How does the fatherhood experience of David sharpen the meaning of these words for us?

# Job

Job is in a class by himself. His story is both remarkable and familiar. His name has proverbial status in Western culture and is usually associated with untiring patience—which is a bit odd, actually, since patience is neither the point of the book nor a virtue exceptionally evidenced in Job. There are different, more important, themes at work in story of Job.

Still, for all the profundity and power at work in the book, Job is not exactly a critical figure in Israel's unfolding history. Job is not part of the kingly line; he is not numbered among the patriarchs. His father and his sons are virtually irrelevant to the story of the people of Israel—the Bible doesn't even bother to record their names. It seems that no one who matters is descended from Job. Scholars are not even certain where or when he lived. No covenant promises are made to Job. There are no visions of apocalyptic judgment and no prophetic discourses calling people to repentance in the book. Anyone who has read just a part of the book that bears Job's name realizes that it is not so much a story as a question asked over the course of about thirty-five chapters of vivid and potent poetry. This is the strength and the timeless attraction of the book. This is what puts Job in a class by himself. Job asks aloud the question that recurs in every generation: why? Why does God let good people suffer? Why does God not answer heartfelt prayers for mercy? Why does God do things that seemingly make no sense? Why?

The most unsettling and significant questions of theology—perhaps of human existence—are explored in the Book of Job. The problem of suffering, the meaning of earthly life, the relationship between Creator and creature, the limits of human comprehension, the existence of evil and a permissive God—these are the concerns at work in the story of Job. This also raises yet another legitimate question: what is a heavy subject like Job doing in an unpretentious study on fatherhood that didn't provide a warning about the possibility of an occasional foray into the impenetrable depths of serious theology? Before crying "foul!" relax; this is not a bit of theological bait and switch. Nor has the mission been forgotten. The assigned topic is still in sight, and the temptation to mine the depths will be resisted, or mostly resisted.

It is hard to ignore the big questions when they are the center of attention in the Book of Job. Besides, a fair amount of heavy theology has already found its way into previous chapters (even if you may not have realized it), and you survived that in good shape. But, for the moment, the focus is fatherhood. And while it may be little more than a sideshow to the main event in Job, in the midst of fantastic existential and theological reflection, the story of Job still offers important instruction about the basic work of a father.

Introducing Job's family is not difficult. He has a wife, who plays a minimal role. In fact, she makes only one appearance, but she exploits it and seals her place in biblical lore. After Job had lost all his possessions (including the yet-to-be-introduced children), was afflicted with head-to-toe sores, and took up residence on the ash heap with his potsherd scraper for his lesions, his wife makes her debut and delivers her line: "Do you still hold fast your integrity? Curse God and die!" That's it. After Job's subsequent reprimand of his wife, we never hear from her or about her again. So, Job's wife becomes synonymous with the well-timed word of encouragement. Perhaps she deserves her reputation, or perhaps her words were actually taken out of context, or maybe she was having a bad day. At any rate, she succeeds in adding to Job's burden.

But this is not a study on biblical wives, so it is time to return to the rest of Job's family: seven sons and three daughters, totaling a perfect ten. Between his idealized family and his extraordinary wealth, Job was the "greatest of all the people of the east" (Job 1:3). But his true greatness was not immediately evident.

Job's sons had a regular routine of week-long feasting. With seven brothers, it was an easy pattern; each of the seven would host the family gathering on his allotted day of the week. The text doesn't provide any detail about the week of feasting; it's possible that those seven successive gatherings were as innocent and wholesome as the average American family's Thanksgiving dinner. But it's also possible that, at least on occasion, the movable feast looked less like a family meal and more like a pub crawl. This supposition gains credence in light of Job's own regular practice. At the end of the week of feasting, Job would offer sacrifices on behalf of each child. "For Job said, 'It may be that my children have sinned and cursed God in their hearts' " (Job 1:5). Like every faithful Christian father, Job was moved by two great loves—his love for his children and his love for God. It was his concern for his children and the relationship that each had with God that prompted his commitment to intervene for them on a regular basis—especially when he had reason for anxiety.

Job's solicitude for his children is immediately familiar. We recognize it in countless Christian parents who agonize over the choices and behaviors of their children, who pray ceaselessly for those children, and who would do anything to ensure that those children would walk always uprightly in true faith. This is not a quaint or sentimental attitude worthy only of churchly old grandmothers who don't understand the world today. The desire to see one's children remain in a vibrant and formative relationship with God should define every parent. Nothing matters more. And the cornerstone of this noble preoccupation is the ardent prayer that a father continually offers for his children. In the midst of soccer practice, math tutoring, science project coaching, college saving, and practicing politeness, don't forget the most important thing. Pray for your children. Pray for their faithfulness. Pray for their salvation. Pray with regularity and determination.

But don't stop there. Add to your faithful, fatherly praying a faithful and righteous life that models the sort of life you want your children to live. This is what Job did. He was "the greatest person in the east," not because of his wealth or blessings, but because of his righteous character. Job lived with integrity. Job lived with consistency. Job lived faithfully. What Job's children heard from their father, they saw in their father. There was no disparity between his words and his deeds. He backed his regular intercession for his children with a life fully dedicated to God's will and purposes. Job gave his sons and daughters the reliable, routine, and relentless embodiment of a holy life. A father can give no greater gift to his children.

In the last verses of Job, we are given one more glimpse into Job's character and his unflinching dedication to his children. Part of the restoration of Job's fortunes was a new set of seven sons and three daughters. We are even given the names of three of these children—the daughters. Apparently, they were worthy of specific mention. No ordinary girls, for "in all the land there were no women so beautiful as Job's daughters" (Job 42:15). The truly remarkable thing, though, is that Job honors these daughters and proves the extent of his fatherly concern by granting them inheritance rights along with their brothers. Job breaks with cultural practices and societal expectations simply for the sake of doing what is right for his own family. Job loves his children with impartiality and consistency. Living his righteousness begins at home, as it should.

In a sense, of course, Job as model father is only a tangent to the real story. Truthfully, in the book, Job's original ten children serve as a plot device for Job's tragedy. Their party routine provides an easy target for Satan's lethal cyclone. It is the sudden and comprehensive extinction of his progeny that matters. We learn about his children so that we can grieve with Job when he loses them. And we learn about their habit of feasting so that we might gain a deeper appreciation of the character of Job when we see him interceding for them. Job is a model parent. Indeed, Job is a model everything. He's doing things right. That's the point. The reader must know that Job is "a blameless and upright man, who fears God and turns away from evil" (Job 1:8), or the rest of the story loses all of its poignant impact.

The crux of the issue at work in the Book of Job is precisely the fact that Job is a good—indeed a *righteous*—guy who does everything the way it should be done. And he suffers horrifically anyway.

It doesn't add up. It makes no sense. Why would God do this to Job? This is the preoccupation and recurrent theme of the book. The question is sweeping and universal in scope and certainly relevant to a man striving to excel in his role of father. Why is it that a good man who strives to do the right things for his family nevertheless suffers grave injustice and great pain? Job wants an answer. He is determined to hold God accountable: "I would speak to the Almighty, and I desire to argue my case with God" (Job 13:3). Who can blame Job for his confusion and indignation over the gross injustice that had ruined him?

Actually, his friends could. In rich and potent epic poetry, Job's three friends hint, suggest, and accuse the pathetic man of deserving what he was getting. And with poetic flourish equal to that of his friends, Job insists with untiring tenacity that he is innocent and undeserving of the tragic ordeal that had been imposed on him. This is the outline of chapters 4–31. After six more chapters where the youth Elihu upbraids all of his elders, including Job, for speaking rashly and erroneously about God and his justice, Job finally gets his wish, and God answers his question. Well, not exactly. God speaks—even directly—to Job. But God does not answer Job's consuming, accusing question. He never tells Job or us why. Instead, for two solid chapters (and two more after that), God calls Job to account. "Where were you when I laid the foundation of the earth? . . . Have you commanded the morning since your days began? . . . Have you comprehended the expanse of the earth? . . . Can you lead forth the Mazzaroth in their season?" (Job 38:4, 12, 18, 32). The Lord is relentless and overwhelming. When at last He pauses and demands a response from Job, the righteous man has gotten the message: "Behold, I am of small account; what shall I answer you? I lay my hand on my mouth. I have spoken once, and I will not answer; twice, but I will proceed no further" (Job 40:4–5).

This is a hard lesson, and we creatures are notoriously slow to learn it and frighteningly quick to forget it. Whether we like it or not, and usually we don't like it, we are but creatures and cannot call our Creator to task or even impose on him our ideas about what is fair or just. That was the point of God's remarkable series of questions to Job. Essentially, God was saying, "Okay, Job, exactly who do you think you are? Are you really prepared to challenge your Creator and Judge about what is good or right?"

Having heard God's response, Job did the one and only wise thing that he could do. "I had heard of You by the hearing of the ear, but now my eye sees You; therefore I despise myself, and repent in dust and ashes" (Job 42:5–6). Face-to-face with God, creatures can only repent. They cannot bargain. They cannot demand. They cannot argue. They cannot expect. They can only repent. Being a righteous man, Job did the right thing. He repented. His days of demanding an answer were done. His indignant challenge to God for an explanation was renounced. His expectation of a holy hearing in which to plead his case was forgotten. Everything was swallowed by the reality of a holy God who was the supreme Creator and Master of everything—including Job.

Job asks the "why" questions that lie at the heart of all human suffering. The questions are still asked today. And, the friends of Job with their reasonable but woefully wrong answers are still offering their help today. Like those misguided friends, people today are still intent on making God make sense, and providing rational explanations for the suffering and evil in the world. Their solutions number too many to count, much less mention. Endlessly creative, creatures never tire of the exercise and try to devise some system, some explanation that will answer the questions and soothe our troubled minds with a reasonable solution. But it can't be done. Job's friends and their errant efforts incurred God's keen rebuke: "My anger burns against you . . . for you have not spoken of Me what is right, as My servant Job has" (Job 42:7).

Once again, Job found himself in the role of intercessor, this time pleading for the sake of his three friends who sinned against God. It is remarkable and somewhat startling to our usual way of thinking. The friends' attempts to explain God and his actions are judged more offensive than Job's sobbing and his cries of unfairness. Job's friends were wrong to presume to know the ways of God. Job, on the other hand, simply expressed the perplexity of his heart without claiming to understand what God was doing or why.

In the end, the story of Job probably leaves us asking even more questions than before the story began. In fact, the story of Job generates many questions and offers few, if any, straight answers. And that's fine. In fact, that's good. Job is not given to us to satisfy our curiosity or to provide a neat system for analyzing the reasons for suffering or evil in any given situation. Instead, in Job we are confronted with the one answer, the one reality, the one truth that does matter. We are compelled to recognize and admit again that we are only creatures—but creatures being cared for by a God who is eminently more wise and more loving than we could ever hope to comprehend. How could we understand? We are but creatures—creatures with definite and determined limits on their understanding, creatures who always have more questions than they have answers. Job teaches us to learn to be creatures and to be content with that. If we creatures of the twenty-first century could learn just this much, it would revolutionize and reshape every layer of our culture. Perhaps that is hoping for too much. Indeed, it would be no small thing if in our churches, if in our *own* lives, we could learn this lesson. The impact on our churches, our own lives, and the lives of our children would be no less revolutionary—and no less exciting. To live as a creature, faithfully doing what his Creator has given him to do, to trust the Creator and His plan even when it makes absolutely no sense to us, to cling to the Creator's grace even when it has been obscured by evil and is impossible to see, this is the beautiful lesson to be learned from the life of Job.

In His mercy, the Creator restored Job's many blessings that He had, without cause or explanation, once so cavalierly taken from Job. It would be one more mistake of human logic to assume that God will do the same for all who suffer injustice and pain in spite of their faithful service. Sometimes the resolution doesn't come, at least not that we can see. But what we can see is what God has promised, what Job was able to see from a distance by faith: "For I know that my Redeemer lives, and at the last He will stand upon the earth. And after my skin has been thus destroyed, yet in my flesh I shall see God" (Job 19:25–26). Such is the hope and the certainty of all creatures who, like Job, cling to the promise of their Redeemer, Jesus Christ.

## Questions

1. Children often ask very thoughtful and difficult questions. What is one of the most difficult or memorable questions you have heard from a child?

2. In your own life, what questions are most troubling to you?

3. Three times Job is described as "blameless and upright, one who feared God and turned away from evil" (Job 1:1, 8; 2:3). And we are told, "In all this Job did not sin." Given that all men are sinners and unrighteous, how are we to understand these claims?

4. Read Job 1:6–12. Without getting distracted by the unanswerable oddity of Satan's presence in God's throne room, what does this background to the story of Job teach about the reasons for Job's imminent suffering?

5. Read Job 16:6–14. While Satan orchestrates Job's suffering (Job 2:1–6), Job places the blame elsewhere. Is Job right? How do you reconcile his complaint with chapters 1–2 of the book?

6. Leaving behind questions without easy answers, what do you think is the most important thing that Job does for his children?

7. What would Job's habit of interceding for his children look like today? What kinds of things should be included in your prayers for your children?

8. How might regular prayer for your children affect your parenting?

9. It was noted in the study that one of Job's great gifts to his children was the example of a life lived faithfully and piously. Do you agree with this? How important is a father's example for the shaping of his children?

10. Read Job 19:23–27 and 40:1–5. Do these statements from Job contradict or support one another? What comfort is there in the answer Job finally accepts?

# Solomon

The acorn never falls far from the oak tree. An exhaustive familiarity with Western proverbs is certainly not necessary for one to recognize the truth in this aphorism. Like any good proverb, the validity of the saying is immediately verified by personal experience. It rings true. Like father, like son. Whether genetics or environment, breeding or upbringing, however it is said, the truth remains. A father has a profound impact on the shaping of his child. In this study, ample evidence has already been presented in our consideration of the fathers who have gone before. But now, we come to the ancient master of proverbs, Solomon himself. And, as we shall see, Solomon gives us some reason to wonder about the veracity of the proverb about acorns and oaks.

Any account of the great men of the Old Testament would be woefully incomplete without Solomon. His name became synonymous with virtually every superlative that matters. Forever after, Solomon set the bar for wisdom, wealth, prestige, influence, royal administration, national building projects, and success—both personal and political. Yet, Solomon's place on the roster of courageous biblical fathers is hardly a foregone conclusion. Indeed, if it actually came to a debate, one might stand a better chance of coming out on top by arguing against Solomon's listing. The biblical record leaves us with an impression of Solomon that is ambivalent at best. And it is precisely the checkered legacy of Solomon that makes the great king such a fascinating character and such a worthy subject of our careful consideration. How the wisest and best could father the sort of son who succeeds him on the throne; how a man with the faith and humility to pray only for wisdom to rule could disparage his heritage and collapse in the foulest apostasy—these are puzzles that should command our attention.

In Proverbs and Ecclesiastes, the Bible preserves for us a fair sampling of Solomon's great wisdom and some of his three thousand wise sayings (1 Kings 4:32). Not surprisingly, Solomon speaks often about fathers and parenting and offers eloquent exhortations to parents and to children, including this gem: "A wise son makes a glad father, but a foolish son is a sorrow to his mother" (Proverbs 10:1).

Indeed, the saying rings with self-evident truth. But, ironically, in the case of the apothegm's creator, we are left to wonder exactly where Solomon came out on this one. Was Solomon the sort of son who would have made David glad? Given Solomon's celebrated wisdom, no father should have been gladder than David.

Still, by the time Solomon's life story had finally run its course, the evaluation of his life had become decidedly more complicated, and it is not hard to imagine Bathsheba shedding tears of grief over what her beloved son had become. He squandered the spiritual inheritance gained from his father, and the legacy he left his own heirs bore no resemblance to the one he had once gained. Perhaps this best accounts for the virtual absence of Solomon's name from future accounts of Israel's greatness. It was not the man, but only the temple that bore the man's name, that was remembered with unsullied joy. Solomon's story is not what it should have been. Solomon attained great heights in virtually every realm, yet his story ends in bitter division and hollow, aching sorrow.

Things began well. Just before his death, David, in an unusual move of domestic engagement, took decisive action on behalf of has favored son and assured Solomon's succession to the throne of Israel (1 Kings 1). The new king followed the deathbed advice of his seasoned father to the letter and firmly established himself as king (1 Kings 2). David set his son on the right path, and Solomon was following that path. "Solomon loved the LORD, walking in the statutes of David his father" (1 Kings 3:3).

At this ripe moment, God made his famous offer to Solomon, "Ask what I shall give you" (1 Kings 3:5). Solomon made his famous reply, assuring his course toward greatness: "Give Your servant therefore an understanding mind to govern Your people, that I may discern between good and evil" (1 Kings 3:9).

Armed with his wise and discerning mind—gifts from God graciously given to one who treasured true humility—Solomon began his remarkable reign. He proved an able ruler, with the borders of Israel stretching to their widest bounds. "Solomon ruled over all the kingdoms from the Euphrates to the land of the Philistines and to the border of Egypt" (1 Kings 4:21). For his entire reign, Solomon and his people prospered in perfect peace.

Of course, his rule was also noteworthy for his incomparable wisdom. The biblical description of Solomon's wisdom spares no superlative: "Solomon's wisdom surpassed the wisdom of all the people of the east and all the wisdom of Egypt. For he was wiser than all other men" (1 Kings 4:30–31). Such wisdom had its material reward, manifest in palace tableware of pure gold. "None were of silver; silver was not considered as anything in the days of Solomon" (1 Kings 10:21). Solomon was living large.

Living large is not a sin—at least not *necessarily* a sin. And there are some superlatives one may pursue and enjoy without peril—faith and wisdom being paramount examples. But Solomon took his superlative, living-large mentality and applied it not only to his wisdom, his kingdom, his worship, and his wealth, but also to his wife (or rather, wives).

David, you remember, had been challenged with a disability when it came to saying no to women. The principle of fatherly influence holds yet again; the acorn sprouted and rooted within the shadow of the oak before eclipsing it. Solomon took David's foible and with careful cultivation nurtured this liability to a breathtaking extreme. Wife number one had been a sensational catch. There were only so many daughters of Pharaoh, and Solomon married one of them. But in addition to that first wife, there were another 699. That's right, Solomon had seven hundred (that's *seven hundred*) wives—one for each day for almost two years. And, just in case he tired of them, his harem had another three hundred concubines (1 Kings 11:3).

Perhaps it goes without saying, but this was not a good thing. It is worth remembering that when God established marriage, it was one man and one woman becoming one flesh (Genesis 2:24). Polygamy might have been practiced—even by the patriarchs— but it was not God's intent. A biblical report of a man's deed should

73

not be construed as divine endorsement of the deed. Next to Solomon, David's bevy of wives seems altogether moderate. Still, David had been guilty of ignoring the clear word from the Pentateuch forbidding kings to multiply wives (Deuteronomy 17:17). Solomon made an absolute mockery of the mandate, flaunting not only its prohibition against acquiring multiple wives, but rejecting as well the verse's further warning against acquiring excessive silver and gold. In the case of Solomon, the result was exactly what had been predicted: his heart was turned away (1 Kings 11:4). And the God who once had blessed Solomon so spectacularly now rejected him. "And the LORD was angry with Solomon, because his heart had turned away from the LORD, the God of Israel. . . . Therefore the LORD said to Solomon, 'Since this has been your practice and you have not kept My covenant and My statutes that I have commanded you, I will surely tear the kingdom from you and will give it to your servant'" (1 Kings 11:9–11).

Generations later, after Israel had been fractured, eroded, besieged, scattered, exiled, and finally minimally restored, Nehemiah was actually able to use Solomon as an example—a negative example. "Did not Solomon king of Israel sin on account of such women? Among the many nations there was no king like him, and he was beloved by his God, and God made him king over all Israel. Nevertheless, foreign women made even him to sin" (Nehemiah 13:26).

Nehemiah's point is arresting and apropos. If Solomon, with all of his wisdom and all of his divine favor and all of his advantages of birth, was still subject to spiritual disaster, then how much more are we? Of course, for Nehemiah and his first audience, the lesson of Solomon was even more pointed. His constituents were making precisely the same error as the once-great king. They were marrying "foreign women," that is, women who were not daughters of Israel, women who did not worship Yahweh. It would be naive and ultimately foolish to apply Nehemiah's lesson too narrowly: "I only have one wife, and she's not a foreigner, so . . ."

Clearly, the harsh lesson of Solomon's life is more broadly applicable than simply to choose well when you marry and to limit that choice to one. Though, of course, as we saw with the great concern of both Abraham and Isaac over the selection of wives for their sons, one should not dismiss the importance even of this obvious application. But the real point of Solomon's story is the need of every father—every man—to keep humility before the Creator and a trust in His Word as the foundation and direction of life. In what mattered most, Solomon failed.

Exactly what sort of dynamics were at work between the generations in the household of David we can only guess—which is, of course, a fool's occupation. But the outcome is clear. David died in faith and left the legacy of a man after God's own heart. Solomon died in disgrace (at least from God's perspective) and left a legacy tarnished and confused at best. Solomon reminds us that a life can be evaluated only when seen complete. Seen that way, David shines, while Solomon is diminished and ultimately dismissed. There is no easy way to account for this. Did the father's instruction extend to his son? Did the acorn, indeed, grow close to the oak? In some ways, the influence of David is obvious in his son—he inherited many of the same besetting temptations. But, the one thing that mattered most, faith in God and His Word, was lost in the handoff between generations.

The break between the next generations was even more marked. While the overall assessment of Solomon is decidedly negative, he at least governed with wisdom and accomplished much for the nation. Rehoboam succeeded him, the only son of Solomon ever mentioned—although with one thousand wives and concubines, one has to wonder. Rehoboam was arrogant and ignorant and too full of his self-delusion to recognize either fault. Ignoring the counsel of his father's wise elders, he followed the flattery of his peers, rejected his oppressed subjects' appeal for leniency in their work, alienated ten of Israel's tribes, fomented civil war, and ultimately shattered the kingdom forever. There's no doubt where Rehoboam comes out in the judgment of the proverb: he's a fool who gives his mother sorrow.

Solomon's son has already received more attention than he deserves. More vital to our learning is the enigma of Solomon. It is not difficult to discern a progression in the life of Solomon, a progression from vibrant faith to a heart "turned away." What accounts for that turn may be less apparent and might spark some degree of bewilderment. Of course, as we've already noted, the Bible itself indicts Solomon's outlandish collection of foreign wives. We need look no further for an adequate explanation. Still, there are lingering perplexities, and it is intriguing to notice a potential correlation between Solomon's shifting wisdom and his fall from faith. In the beginning, even before his petition for wisdom, Solomon displayed exceptional understanding, willingly acknowledging his own inadequacy and limitations: "You have made Your servant king in place of David my father, although I am but a little child. I do not know how to go out or come in" (1 Kings 3:7). Armed with a humble spirit and God's greater gift of wisdom, Solomon dazzled his people and the nations around.

The practical wisdom of Solomon is evident in the Book of Proverbs. The book provides outstanding counsel, much of it powerfully directed from father to son.

> Hear, O sons, a father's instruction, and be attentive, that you may gain insight. . . . When I was a son with my father . . . he taught me and said to me, "Let your heart hold fast my words; keep my commandments, and live."
>
> Proverbs 4:1–4

When he delivered the wisdom contained in Proverbs, Solomon was aware of the critical importance of the generational handoff of wisdom and character. How odd—and how sobering—that the handoffs on either end of Solomon's life were ultimately botched. David's legacy of faith, Solomon denigrated. And the wisdom that defined Solomon found no quarter in the court of Rehoboam. Still, Proverbs proves that at one point in his life, Solomon's wisdom was turned to the affairs of everyday living, and he offered guidance that people continue to ponder and treasure.

And then there's Ecclesiastes. Aside from the lyrical verses of chapter 3 detailing "a time for every matter under heaven" (v. 1), the tone and teaching of Ecclesiastes is not exactly bright or uplifting. "Vanity of vanities! All is vanity" (Ecclesiastes 1:2). "So I hated life, because what is done under the sun was grievous to me, for all is vanity and a striving after wind" (2:17).

There are many important nuances, of course, and one can recognize an unflinching honesty at work in the chapters of Ecclesiastes that holds its own attraction, but there is little doubt that Ecclesiastes betrays a jaded, or at least a harshly realistic, perspective on life not present in Proverbs. One might even argue that in Ecclesiastes, pessimism has taken over. Perhaps it has. But pessimism is not necessarily a sin, and even those blessed with personalities that favor a half-empty negativity might still confess the promises of Christ.

For Solomon, though, pessimism was only a point along his downward slide to what finally became despair, idolatry, and apostasy. Which one has primacy is unclear and unimportant. They go hand in hand. It is a sharp warning to check the pull of pessimism and to cling to what God has revealed. A man has a responsibility to monitor the attitude and perspective that animates and defines his being and his living. A Pollyanna outlook is not required (or even desired), but neither can one allow cynicism and healthy realism to become excuses for lack of faith and entrées for idols. Solomon's precipitous downward spiral stands as stark testimony.

The story should have been one to celebrate—Israel's great king leaves the throne in the hands of his great son; David establishes a dynasty that grows stronger and grander as it passes into the hands of Solomon, the wisest of all men. But what should have been is not what was. Solomon's spectacular wisdom was no hedge against self-destruction—perhaps it precipitated it. The dynasty would not achieve the dream of an everlasting reign. The nation would not flourish under the wise and just rule of a succession of Davidic potentates. Eventually, it would all end in national and spiritual disaster. Such is the inevitable harvest of human wisdom that scorns humility and disdains its source.

Yet, even when David's sons failed, God did not forget David or his promise to the shepherd-king. Solomon did not fulfill the promised expectations. Another would have to do that. Another *did* do that. Great David's greater Son arrived at last, and the promise was realized. Jesus Himself said it, "Behold, something greater than Solomon is here" (Matthew 12:42). Indeed, Solomon's Creator was here; David's Lord was present. This Son surpassed every superlative and every achievement of Solomon. This Son of David, the one true Son of David, reestablished the Davidic dynasty, but in a way no one had anticipated. It was founded not on military prowess, administrative brilliance, human resilience, or rational ingenuity. It was built on divine forgiveness, love, and grace. This is the only foundation that endures. This is—*He* is—the only foundation sufficient for building a dynasty or a family.

# Questions

1. Who is the wisest person you have known or met? What makes you consider him or her so wise?

2. Read 1 Kings 3:3–14. Using relevant portions of the text to support your thoughts, describe Solomon as he appears in these verses.

3. Read Ecclesiastes 9:1–10. What is the tone of Solomon's counsel? What is your reaction to his observations? How does this fit with your understanding of the way a Christian is to live?

4. At what point does healthy and honest realism change into cynicism and even despair? How does one guard against becoming jaded about life and even religion?

5. Read 1 Kings 11:1–13. It is commonly said that one of the best ways a father can love his children is by loving his wife. What do you think of this idea? Does it hold true with Solomon? How does a man's marriage impact his children and his whole life?

6. Read Proverbs 1:1–10. Based on these verses, how would you define wisdom? What is the relationship between wisdom and morality?

7. How much of parenting amounts to the exercise of wisdom? Where can a man turn to find wisdom for his role and work as father?

8. What danger might there be in relying too much on the wisdom that one has acquired? In light of Solomon's story, what restraints (if any) should be placed on the exercise of wisdom?

9. How might it be possible for intellectualism or rationalism to masquerade as wisdom but finally collapse into idolatry? Can you think of any contemporary examples?

10. Read Proverbs 22:6. Given the sorry tale of Solomon and his unfortunate heir, how are we to understand this verse? Is there any way to ensure that a father to son handoff is not botched?

# Joseph

You know right where to find him. Every December, he gets his staff, and sometimes a lantern, and takes his spot in the stable next to the manger. He's usually standing, while Mary kneels a bit closer to the infant. But he's got his place, right in the middle of things, there in the crèche. Joseph is a standard part of the Christmas story and our celebration of Christmas. But, Joseph is not the main attraction. The Baby, of course, is the center of attention. Even Mary overshadows Joseph and has the next place of honor—sometimes, even often, she is holding the Child, and Joseph drops out of the scene completely—it's just Madonna and Child and no Joseph. But, as we shall see, this wouldn't have bothered Joseph in the least. Joseph was never one to steal a scene. He knew his place.

While he is almost certainly the most familiar father of the New Testament, he's not the first; Zechariah (father of John the Baptizer) has that distinction. Joseph doesn't join the ranks of biblical fathers until later—some would say *much* later. Actually, including Joseph as a biblical father raises interesting questions. Christian confession is clear: Mary is the true human mother of Jesus, but Jesus' father is only the heavenly Father. Scripture stresses this point often: no human father is involved. The virgin birth is an important and familiar article of our faith, but we might not have given much thought to the implications of this teaching, particularly for the man in the manger scene.

We can call him a stepfather, or the supposed father, of Jesus, but Joseph is not Jesus' father. Many Christians throughout history go even further in undermining Joseph's hold on fatherhood, believing that Joseph never did father any of his own children. The teaching of the perpetual virginity of Mary holds that not only was Mary a virgin when she gave birth to Jesus, but that she remained a virgin for the rest of her life. Martin Luther held this position, as did most of his contemporaries. Obviously, Joseph would not have been unaffected, giving us even more reason, perhaps, to call him St. Joseph. In the case of the perpetual virginity, he earned the title.

Without getting bogged down in a lengthy discussion about the extent of Mary's virginity after Jesus' birth, it is enough to note that the central truths of Christianity are not altered in the least if, after Jesus' birth, Mary and Joseph had honored God's will expressed in the garden and had more children. The natural reading of Scripture supports the idea (Matthew 13:55), and it is good to remember that God does not privilege virginity above motherhood. But, even if Joseph did eventually join the ranks of biblical fathers the usual way, our interest is in what we know about his role as the earthly father of Jesus. On this topic, we are not limited to mere speculation. The Bible, in the Gospels of Matthew and Luke, provides with some detail a record of the events preceding and including Jesus' birth. And in these stories, Joseph is a critical character. You remember the stories. Angels, surprise pregnancy, shifting wedding plans, nighttime flights from tyrants, shepherds and Magi from the east—the Christmas story is part of our history and even part of our Western culture. But, again, we might not have considered the story from the perspective of the surrogate father.

Obviously, Joseph knew there was something extraordinary about the Child being carried by his betrothed. He had been told so during a dream-visit by an angel (Matthew 1:21), corroborating the story that he had no doubt already heard from Mary herself. And then, there were the following remarkable events during those early days in Bethlehem: shepherds appearing and worshiping at the manger, incredible words of prophecy about their Baby from wizened seers in the Jerusalem temple, lavish gifts from foreign scholars, another angel-laden dream, and a dash out of Bethlehem—out of Israel. Nothing was normal about any of this.

Finally, the family settled down in Nazareth and everything settled down with them. No more angels interrupting Joseph's dreams, no more foreigners knocking on the door, no more frantic fleeing for their lives. The silence of the scriptural record argues for the normalcy of these years. But our curiosity is not satisfied with silence, and it is hard to resist wondering what it was like to raise the Son of God.

"Normal" would have meant an apprenticeship for Jesus—long hours spent with his father learning the skills of the first-century building trade. Perhaps, as the years scrolled past and as memoires faded, Joseph began to lose track of the true identity of the son who was at his side. It is not as if Jesus *acted* like God. According to His human nature, He didn't know things before Joseph told Him. He didn't exercise a little divine power as needed to smooth out the bumps in life. Jesus didn't correct Joseph's occasional mistakes by stretching a board cut too short. He didn't conjure cash when a client was slow to pay and things got a bit tight. For all those years, Joseph did what fathers do and raised his son—who was by all appearances an ordinary boy.

Luke breaks the silence to tell us about one incident that happened when Jesus was twelve. It is interesting because it shows two things. According to their regular custom, Joseph led his family south—a journey of several days—to Jerusalem to celebrate the Passover according to divine mandate. On the homeward trip, Joseph and Mary realized they were missing Jesus. (Pilgrims on the way to Passover often traveled in celebratory groups, so it would not have been that odd for a twelve-year-old to be misplaced in the happy commotion.) Mary and Joseph backtracked to the city, searched for Jesus, and finally found Him in the temple calmly listening to Israel's scholars and asking questions.

The first thing that stands out is that if this is the most dramatic and noteworthy occurrence of Jesus' childhood, then it was normal indeed! The second thing to notice is that whatever Joseph might have been thinking, Jesus was not in the dark about His own identity. "Did you not know that I must be in My Father's house?" (Luke 2:49). It's possible that some of the old busybodies in Nazareth might have had some questions about the paternity of Mary's firstborn, but Jesus had no doubt. He knew His father was *the* Father. Jesus might have looked altogether ordinary, but He knew the reality. He knew whose Son He was, and He knew what that was going to mean.

We could speculate endlessly about what Jesus knew when. He is God in the flesh, but He is also a true human who grew and learned like every other human. We wonder what He understood about Himself at age 3 or 12. And, we wonder what it must have been like to live in the same house with Jesus. Could Mary look at her Son without remembering the haunting words of Simeon: "This child is appointed for the fall and rising of many . . . and a sword will pierce through your own soul also" (Luke 2:34–35)?

Did Joseph ever wonder about his own relationship to the Son that was not his own, but who was entrusted to his care? Curiosity about these things is natural, but will never lead us beyond pure conjecture. So, as we've done before, we cling to the text, refocus on the task at hand, and consider what we do have. And, what we do have is a remarkable portrait of the man Joseph. Much is what we expect, but there might also be a surprise or two.

Out of all the potential mothers in the line of Judah, in all the history of Israel, God specifically selected Mary to be the mother of the Messiah. That makes her special. But it also makes the man to whom she was already betrothed special. Mary was picked with Joseph as part of the package. So, by picking Mary, God also picked Joseph. He was chosen for his task, and not surprisingly, he proved, like Mary, to be equal to what was expected of him. In fact, Joseph is the first father we yet have considered who does not have a negative mark on his record. Obviously, the man was not sinless, but neither was he guilty of some vice or failing that drew the rebuke or correction of God. Joseph was a good man. Okay, that's a bit vague and general—but it is true, and perhaps exceptionally rare, to name a man and be free to describe him as *good* without any qualification.

Joseph's exceptional moral character is supported by many specifics from the sacred text. It has already been pointed out that the practice of Jesus' family was an annual Passover pilgrimage to Jerusalem. This habit reflects the character and piety of the father of the family. Whether he intends it or not, every father sets a tone in his family. The tone in Joseph's family was one of consistent piety. By example, Joseph taught his family the importance of worship and careful observance of God's festival of grace. There is a strong parallel here to the countless godly men who establish the habit of weekly worship, no matter what. The piety of Joseph is also revealed in the fact that Jesus' circumcision and Mary's purification both happened by the book, right on schedule (Luke 2:21–24). That Joseph was ready to divorce his mysteriously pregnant betrothed also further indicates the importance he attached to following the law of God, which forbid a man to marry an adulterous woman. Joseph wanted to do things the right way, God's way.

The claim that Joseph is good is also supported by his regular practice of immediate and unhesitating obedience. The morning after his first dream encounter with God's angel, "When Joseph woke from sleep, he did as the angel of the Lord commanded him" (Matthew 1:24). He didn't need to think it over. He didn't need to consult with friends or trusted confidants. He did what he was told to do. The next time an angel interrupted Joseph's dreams, it was urgent. Herod was out to kill the child. Joseph didn't wait for the sun. While it was still night, he packed up his family and left for Egypt, what must have seemed to Joseph a strange country on the other side of the world (Matthew 2:14). Again, Joseph obeyed without objection or question. It was just the way Joseph was, it seems. He did what God wanted him to do.

Joseph's quiet humility also argues for the exemplary character of Jesus' earthly father. That Joseph was a typical man's man is hinted at in the narratives of Jesus' childhood. Apparently, Joseph was more than ready to stay quiet and let his wife do the talking. When Elizabeth blesses Mary and confirms the word of Gabriel, Mary responds with a song—the Magnificat (Luke 1:46–56). Joseph never sings; Joseph never speaks. In fact, Joseph never says a word. After Mary and Joseph finally found in the temple the object of their three-day search, it was Mary who spoke to Jesus: "Your father and I have been searching for You in great distress" (Luke 2:48).

Joseph, it seems, did not have much to say. Quiet humility that issued in action—that was the way of Joseph. He knew he was a stand-in, temporary father. It is not hard to create a fanciful scenario of Joseph in a crisis of identity, questioning his personal significance after Jesus' declaration that He must be in His "Father's house." But, it is more likely that Joseph handled this with typical aplomb. Luke records that "they did not understand the saying that He spoke to them" (Luke 2:50). Given the ordinary way that Jesus was growing up, this is not surprising. Neither Joseph nor Mary could possibly have grasped the full import of the incredible reality in which they were living. Joseph did not need to understand (how could he?). In humility he simply busied himself with what he did understand: protecting and providing for his family.

Joseph was a simple man. He did what he was given to do. He was given the role of father, and he did what a father needs to do. Foremost on this list was the job of protector. Joseph began his work of protecting his family even before he was married. Remember, because he was righteous and did things God's way, he had intended to divorce Mary. Because he was good and kind, and because he wanted to protect Mary, he resolved to handle Mary's apparent infidelity quietly. The quick obedience of Joseph in shepherding his precious family out of Herod's lethal reach has already been noted. Joseph ably fulfilled the job description of protector. And he did not always wait for divine direction. After Herod died and the all clear was issued, Joseph ventured back to Israel. He hastily concluded that Herod's son was no improvement, and he kept moving all the way back to Nazareth in Galilee. Joseph was serious about his task. He took care of his wife and her son.

Fierce commitment to one's children is familiar to most of us. It seems that the mother-bear instinct is innate—at least in mothers. Fathers, on the other hand, have a tendency to lose track of their responsibility, or maybe it's just that they confuse their priorities. It is good to look to Joseph and see again that the role of protector must be held as the top priority. Escape to Egypt was not part of Joseph's life plan. Joseph may have wondered how a Jewish carpenter was going to make a living in the land of the pharaohs. Providing for a family is important, of course, but keeping that family safe trumps all priorities.

Twenty-first-century fathers are still accountable for the protection of their children. Today, though, the threat is not paranoid kings committed to infanticide. Today, the threat is a decadent culture that entices our children to shun restraint and pursue pleasure wherever it can be found. The threat is intellectual elites who enlighten our children to disavow the reality of God and embrace radical materialism and unrestrained rationalism. The threat today is role models who urge our children to embrace their individuality, choose their own identity, and refuse to conform to any norm that is not self-created. The threats in our world are still very real. A father committed to the sacred task of protecting his children cannot relax. There is no room for distraction. No preoccupation is permitted. Vigilance is demanded. He must be as wise, as tenacious, as responsive, as alert as Joseph.

Joseph did his job well. Not as carpenter, but as a husband and father. He had a family to protect—he had the Holy Family to protect. And he protected it. His was a special family, holy indeed. But the holiness was not from Joseph—no matter how faithful he was as a father. And the holiness was not from Mary—though her favored stature is celebrated even in Scripture. No, the Holy Family was holy for only one reason: Jesus was there. It was holy by contact with the Holy One. Joseph did not earn the nimbus that so often encircles his head in sacred art. Like Mary, he had his nimbus only because he had been brought near to Jesus. He had "contact holiness." So do we. Our holiness is never self-generated. It is never our own achievement. It is always derived, a gift. Our holiness comes the way that Joseph's came. It comes by contact with Jesus. When Christ dwells in us through His Word and Sacraments, we are holy. When Christ dwells in our families in Word and action, when families are founded on the work of Christ, when they are families of forgiveness and incubators of grace, then they are holy. What a wonderful task Joseph was given: the protector of God's Holy Family. What a wonderful task a Christian father has been given: the protector of God's holy family.

# Questions

1. If you were to write a job description of fatherhood, what are three things that could not be left off the list?

2. Clearly God thought that he was qualified for it, but Joseph was given an utterly unique task. What do you think would have been the hardest thing about raising the Son of God? What qualities would be necessary for this responsibility?

3. Assuming he had quiet moments to think, what thoughts might have crossed the Joseph's mind when he considered the true identity of the boy he was raising?

4. Read Luke 2:41–52. What do you think is the most unusual aspect of this story? What does the comment in verse 50 tell you about the home life of Mary and Joseph and about the role of Joseph?

5. Read Matthew 2:13–15. What does this short section teach about the importance of obedience? What are some divine directions that need more obedience from fathers today?

6. Why do you suppose the Bible never records a single word from the mouth of Joseph? What do you think is the greater mistake, a father who talks too much or one who talks too little?

7. Do you agree that a father's greatest responsibility is to protect his family? Why is it that fathers seem able to forget this priority so easily?

8. What are some of the greatest threats to children today? How can a father protect his children from them?




9. What's the difference between being humble and being a pushover? Are strong leadership and humility antithetical? What insight does the example of Joseph provide?




10. What concrete action will you take in the coming week to better fulfill your responsibility as a father?

# Jairus

He knew what he needed to do. There was no question. There was no debate. There was no option. He was out of options. His last hope, his only hope, was Jesus. It was desperation that drove Jairus, and it was love that drove Jairus. His only daughter was dying. He could not save her, and no doctor could save her. But he knew who could save her, or he hoped he knew who could. Out of love for his child, aware of his own crippling helplessness to save the life of his child, Jairus had to find Jesus.

Like so many characters in the Gospel accounts, Jairus appears with minimal introduction and then disappears again without further explanation or subsequent hints about his further life story. So, once again, restraint will be necessary to avoid the real temptation of venturing beyond the words of Scripture into the fanciful world of embellishment and speculation. But we do know a few things about Jairus. His story is told by the first three Gospel writers: Matthew (9:18–26); Mark (5:22–43); and Luke (8:41–56).

In all three, he is described as a ruler of the synagogue. This did not make him a rabbi or a pastor. Being ruler of the synagogue meant that he was responsible for the functioning of the synagogue, making certain all was in order for the weekly services. It would fall to Jairus to arrange for the exposition of Scripture. He would have been the one to invite Jesus to speak on those occasions when Jesus was present at the Capernaum synagogue. And we know that Jairus had a twelve-year-old daughter who was dying.

Well, that's the story as told by Mark and Luke. Matthew devotes less space to this narrative and so condenses the story into half as many verses. Matthew gives us the bottom line—the dying daughter died before Jesus could reach her side. This difference in the three Gospels is not evidence of contradiction, but evidence of the reality that the evangelists each told the story of Jesus' ministry to serve the purpose of this particular Gospel account. It's not unlike the way that reporters will tell the same story in sometimes very different ways.

What little we know of Jairus is enough to foster some fascinating reflection. Capernaum was Jesus' adopted hometown. On the Sea of Galilee, it was the home of several of the disciples, including Peter, James, and John. Jesus based His early ministry in this fishing town. He preached in the synagogue (or synagogues; it's possible Capernaum may have had more than one), He healed those who were sick and demon-possessed, He taught with parables, and He stirred controversy. It was His habit of healing on the Sabbath that ostensibly fueled the conflict. After one of those ill-timed miracles, the opposition crystallized. "The Pharisees went out and immediately held counsel with the Herodians against Him, how to destroy Him" (Mark 3:6). This was not the first sign of trouble. Forgiving the sins of the paralytic who had appeared through the roof agitated the scribes (Mark 2:6–7), and picking grain on the Sabbath got the Pharisees fired up (Mark 2:23–24).

All this happened in and around Capernaum—perhaps right in Jairus's own synagogue. He was in the thick of it. Since the text does not designate him as one, Jairus probably wasn't a Pharisee, but as the ruler of the synagogue, he certainly would have worked closely with and may well have admired the zeal of these ardent, religiously faithful men. Obviously, scribes were also well respected in the synagogue. It requires no conjecture to suggest that Jairus would have had good reason to harbor mixed feelings about Jesus. Those who had earned places of respect and prestige in his circles vocally opposed Jesus. Though Jesus' miracles and teaching were wowing the masses, the more circumspect were at least cautious. There's nothing surprising about this. The pattern is familiar. Even if Jairus was not himself a critic of Christ, he knew people who were, and they were men of stature and significance in his world.

We should take note that we are introduced to Jairus scrambling through the crowds, jostling his way through the crush of bodies, striving to be one of the few who could secure the attention of Jesus. This is hardly typical behavior for a respected ruler of the synagogue. Knowing what we do of the potential "Jesus tensions" at work among the synagogue elite makes Jairus's words and actions more remarkable. He was taking risks seeking Jesus. What he does next is mind-boggling: "Falling at Jesus' feet, he implored Him to come to his house" (Luke 8:41). What an image. Jairus has abandoned all decorum, all calculation, all self-preservation. He is the object lesson of abject humility. Given the urgency of Jairus's predicament, his self-deprecating course seems altogether appropriate. A man will do anything to help his child. For Jairus, the Jesus question was no longer theoretical or academic. It was utterly personal. His daughter was at stake. For her sake, he would willingly cast himself at the feet of Jesus and beg. Dying daughter or not, the reality is that the posture of Jairus is the only possible posture when in the presence of Jesus. Humility is always the beginning.

Jairus trusts Jesus. Again, given the alternative—stay home and watch his daughter die—there may be nothing spectacular in this crisis faith. But Jairus is tenacious and clings to his new Savior. It did not take long for his fledgling faith to be challenged.

It could not have been far to the home of Jairus. Capernaum was not a large city. Travel, though, was maddeningly difficult. Too many people, most not so different from Jairus, wanted something from Jesus. How Jairus responded to the press of moving obstacles we are not told, but it takes little imagination to guess his thoughts. Slow going was excruciating enough, but then everything stopped dead so Jesus could sort things out with a woman bent under her own impossible burden of misery and suffering. For Jairus and his daughter, time was critical. Jairus knew this keenly. Yet again, Jairus was helpless. He could only stand and wait. But he was waiting for Jesus, and his faith did not falter.

Even when the servants arrived with bad news—sent, no doubt, to retrieve the head of the household so that he could attend to his newly imposed responsibilities in the home of a deceased child—Jairus exhibited a blossoming trust. Jesus says, "Do not fear, only believe" (Mark 5:36). Jairus says nothing. He only listens, hopes, and stays with Jesus. Already, Jairus evidences the wisdom of faith.

And when he rejoins and almost certainly embraces his devastated wife, it is not with sorrow and sympathy, but with hope and confidence. It is with Jesus. Out go the frantic, loud mourners—dismissed as quickly as they appeared for so important a family as the synagogue ruler's. In go Jesus, Jairus, his wife, and three select disciples. Then the incredible hope becomes reality. "Little girl, I say to you, arise" (Mark 5:41). And as easily as if she were being awoken at dawn by her mother, the girl rises. The mourners' derisive laughter is shamed into dumbfounded awe. Jairus has his daughter back from the dead, back to stay. Jesus' reminder to give her something to eat assures us of her immediate and complete health.

Jairus did what needed to be done. His priorities were right. Regardless of what others might think, he sought Jesus and pleaded for Jesus to help him. He squelched his pride. He threw himself, literally, on the mercy of Jesus, and he was not disappointed. Jairus understood. He was nothing. Jesus was everything. The crying need of his daughter made the truth starkly clear. Whatever his motives or his doubts or his fears, when he found Jesus, he found all that he needed, all that his daughter needed. He found faith.

Jairus's name is Hebrew and means "God enlightens." Jairus lived up to his name in a way he would never have guessed. His enlightenment did not come after long hours of study or careful instruction or a lifetime of sincere worship. It came when he met Jesus. It came when he learned the profound truth in the words Jesus spoke straight to him: "Fear not, only believe." That was all Jairus needed. When Jesus is the object of belief, then "only believe" is the only thing anyone ever needs.

Jairus ranks as a courageous father because, for the sake of his child, he did what he had to do—at the expense of his own ego and prestige. And he ranks as a courageous father because he models for us the essence of fatherhood rightly conceived and rightly executed. There are three great truths at work in this brief encounter between Jairus and Jesus that teach us much about courageous fatherhood.

First, Jairus teaches a potent and moving lesson about the place of humility. That humility has been a recurrent theme throughout this book is no accident. It could be no other way. Humility before the Creator and Lord is, without exception, the primary posture required of any father. But it was not simply Jairus's terrifying crisis of fatherhood that justified his profound humility. The essential and fundamental necessity of a humble spirit is a truth applicable not only to fathers. It applies to all people. The helpless humility Jairus declared by word and action is the precious confession that must flow from every creature who comes face-to-face with his God. No man saunters into the presence of God with his pockets full of bargaining chips, ready to work a deal. There is no mutuality. There is no reciprocity. Luther was right: we are all beggars. Creatures do not negotiate. They do not bargain. They beg. Jairus embodies this truth.

Humility is always the first position. Everything flows from this foundation. Faith flows from this foundation. And that is the next great truth at work in the story of Jairus: courageous fathers cling to Christ. From humility before Christ always flows faith in Christ. Jairus learned quickly. All he had was Jesus. His only hope was Jesus. All he could do was trust Jesus. For Jairus, this was patently obvious. He had no alternative. Blessed indeed is the man who sees the centrality of his relationship with Christ with such singular focus. Nothing else in creation can supplant Christ. Nothing else can provide what only He can provide. Jesus was all that Jairus had and all that Jairus needed. "Only believe" summed it up beautifully. No deals, no bargains, no extra effort, no other options, only Jesus. Only believe. Courageous fathers—effective, successful fathers—know that uncomplicated trust in the word and work of Jesus is the only thing that matters. Jairus lived this truth. In the face of potential rebuke from peers, in the face of mocking laughter, in the face of death itself, he believed. He kept clinging to Christ.

The encounter between Jairus and Jesus teaches us about the necessity of honest humility and the importance of faith that clings to Christ. It also holds at least one more great truth about the kind of fatherhood to which all men should aspire. It teaches us about the work a father does. Jairus teaches a father that his most important work is to bring Jesus to his children.

In the case of Jairus, this was literally the work he did. He sought Jesus, gained the Savior's attention, won his promise to help, and then led Jesus to the bedside of his daughter. Jairus brought Jesus to his daughter. This is the essential work of every father. Without getting distracted by a pitched debate over who is actually doing the seeking or leading (Scripture and Christian confession are glaringly clear: regardless of our perspective or experience, God is always the one who does the seeking and choosing), there should be consensus on the overriding necessity of a father to lead his children to faith in Jesus. When a father brings his newborn child to the font, he is doing the work of Jairus. He is bringing Jesus to his child. When that same father nurtures the child's faith, reading nightly Bible stories, leading his family to weekly worship, talking about the ways of God to his child in ordinary conversation, living his own life according to God's will, then he continues to bring Jesus to his child. There is much demanded of a father, but there is no task more pressing or more eternally significant than bringing Jesus to his kids.

Much about fatherhood is perplexing and intimidating. How does one get an infant into a onesie without twisting an arm into a position never intended by the Creator? What do you say to comfort a sobbing eleven-year-old in the wake of a best friend's betrayal? How do you encourage a self-conscious adolescent who watches every basketball game from the bench? For a father, the best way forward is not always evident or easy. But the example of Jairus reminds us that there are some things that are explicitly clear and uncomplicated. There's nothing confusing or bewildering about the death of pride. A father may know nothing about cool slumber party dad behavior, but he knows that humility is always right. There's nothing ambiguous about clinging to Christ. Where to turn for solid advice on financing college may be an open question, but unwavering trust in Christ is always a given. And it is obvious that bringing your child to Jesus is the most pressing task set before a man. A guy may not know the right thing to say in the middle of a teen-drama crisis, but he knows that his child needs to hear about Jesus. Perhaps it is wise, especially when fatherhood work is shrouded in mystery and uncertainty, to stop and recall the things that matter. Jairus is an able teacher.

Before we leave Jairus, we should take note of one last thing—probably the most important thing. Maybe it goes without saying, but it would be tragic to assume too much and miss this truth. Jairus burst into the presence of Jesus with the ultimate time-sensitive agenda. He was racing against the clock, racing against death. Time was critical. He hadn't come to realize, yet, that for

Jesus, time is irrelevant. He hadn't learned, yet, that for Jesus, it is never too late. The servants were sure of the sad reality—Jairus's frantic, full-out effort had failed. Jairus knew the truth as well. It was too late. His child was dead. The harsh finality of death destroyed the chance he had begged to obtain. Death crushed all hope. It was too late, but not for Jesus. When Jesus is at work, impossible does not exist.

This truth still holds. Human opinion may draw the inescapable, rational conclusion and declare with solemn certainty the harsh verdict, but Jesus always gets the last word. He is unimpressed with human certainty, rational conclusions, and unflinching facts. Jesus creates His own facts. It was not too late for Jesus. It was not too late for Jairus. It is not too late for you. Maybe your situation is desperate, and you can't imagine what Jesus will be able to do for you. Neither could Jairus. Jesus didn't tell Jairus the plan, He just told Jairus what he needed to know. He tells you the same: "Do not fear, only believe."

## Questions

1. From your own experience, what is one of the most remarkable things you have known a father to do for his child?

2. Read Mark 3:1–6. What does this story have to do with Jairus's initial appeal to Jesus? How do you rate Jairus's initial request to Jesus—is it a prayer of faith, or is something else at work? What was motivating Jairus?

3. Read Mark 5:22–24. Given the attitudes at work among the Jewish leadership and his position of authority in the synagogue, what do you think is the most remarkable thing about Jairus's appeal to Jesus?

4. Read Psalm 51:15–16. How does Jairus's appeal to Jesus reflect his understanding of these verses? What do you think of the assertion that every Christian must begin his life of faith in the same position as Jairus: powerless at the feet of Jesus, seeking God's mercy with nothing to offer?

5. How do people typically respond to the idea that Christianity is founded on the abject helplessness and absolute humility of human beings? Why do you think this is the usual response?

6. Read Mark 5:22–43. How do you think Jairus reacted to the interruption by the suffering woman? What role does the actual course of events play in teaching Jairus about the Christian way of life?

7. All three accounts record the laughter of the mourners. What is significant about the laughter? How might this have affected Jairus and his fledgling faith?

8. Would you say that pride is an asset or a liability when it comes to serving in the role of father? What positive aspects might there be to pride? What are the negative aspects?

9. What keeps a father from being humble before Jesus? How can the pride of a father hinder his ability to care for his children?

10. "Do not fear, only believe" (Mark 5:36). How do you hear these words—are they a challenge or are they comfort?

# The Official

Another sick child, another desperate father, another miracle of grace performed by Jesus—it sounds a bit like a rerun or a contrived plot device that displays little imagination. But the similarities between the story of Jairus and the father whom we'll call the "royal official" are understandable. Yet careful attention to our present story will reveal some significant differences. The story of Jairus was told by Matthew, Mark, and Luke. The story of the royal official is told by John. This fact already signals some marked differences—it also makes it difficult to establish the exact timetable relationship of the two miracles. But none of that matters very much. What matters is that a father comes to Jesus, and Jesus gives him what he seeks—that and much more.

It is not at all surprising that such similar incidents would occur. Jesus' early ministry of teaching and healing was creating a sensation in Israel, and we would expect that as a matter of routine, those in need would flock to Him in the hope of receiving a miracle of their own. This time, it is news of Jesus' return to Galilee after paying a visit to the temple in Jerusalem that prompts a father to action. Jesus is in the hill country of Galilee, in Cana, the same city where He had saved the day for a pair of newlyweds.

But the man with the dying son was not in Cana. He was in Capernaum, almost twenty miles away. But given the chance of saving the life of his son, the distance was immaterial. The royal official covered the ground and appeared before Jesus. We know nothing about the man; this time, we do not even get a name. John simply records that he was an "official" (John 4:46). The text is just that vague. We are left to guess whether this man had blood connections to the house of King Herod, or whether he was merely an official with royal duties. Considering his hometown, the latter is perhaps more likely, but again it matters little. Either way, he is a father of means. He is also a father of helplessness—he needs what only Jesus can give.

So far, the parallel with Jairus is almost complete. But once the quest is successful, the noble father finds Jesus, and the dialogue opens, the present plot bears no resemblance to the previous narrative. Hurrying and hoping to fulfill his mission, this nameless father made his request, and then he made it again . . . and again. He "asked Him to come down and heal his son" (John 4:47). The Greek grammar conveys the idea that this insistent father was repeatedly and persistently making the request of Jesus. We cannot know for sure, but perhaps the scene was not unlike a crowd of reporters all clamoring for the attention of their quarry, hoping their question will be the one that is heard and honored. Or, more worrisome, maybe Jesus heard the request but failed to respond. Whatever the circumstance, the father was tenacious and kept asking.

Finally, the man got Jesus' attention *and* His provocation. Okay, Jesus' words may not be exactly incendiary, but they are hardly encouraging—not what the official, or we, had expected. There's no dodging the truth: Jesus' answer was clipped and barbed with rebuke: "Unless you see signs and wonders you will not believe" (John 4:48). Actually, Jesus had a habit of greeting an earnest inquiry with a response that appears less than enthusiastic. There are some things to note, however.

Jesus speaks to the father, but His words are aimed at a much wider audience. The "you" is plural. Jesus is not singling out the official, but making a general statement, a painful truth about the nature of man. The point seems obvious enough: empirical evidence is what counts for human beings. People often trust what they can see. If it's not amenable to metrics, it's not important. An accomplished miracle beats a someday promise any day. Jesus wants something more. At least for this official, He wants something more. Instead of trusting the miracles and the immediate benefits they give, He wants people to trust the living Word of God. He wants people to trust Him.

As so often in the scriptural record, so it is with the official: Jesus' tepid response does nothing to quell the enthusiasm of his request. As intended, it actually sharpens and intensifies it. Jesus ignores the petition and chides an over-reliance on signs and wonders. The official proves equal to the challenge and for his part ignores the reproach and doggedly pursues his purpose. Oblivious to Jesus' grievance, the anxious father begs one more time: "Sir, [or is it "Lord"?] come down before my child dies" (John 4:49). Human foibles that trouble the Messiah hold no interest for this father—at least not now in the present circumstance. This royal official is not interested in philosophical or theological intricacies. For him, only one thing matters: his son is dying, and he is sure Jesus is his last hope.

Of course, Jesus is neither hard-hearted nor indifferent to the needs of this earnest man. The words of Jesus scold, that is true, but these words are carefully calculated and carefully aimed. They do more than chastise. They call for faith founded not on Jesus' signs, but on Jesus Himself. These words, like all of Christ's words, have their intended effect. The official's incipient faith is forced to grow. In the face of resistance, he will cling all the more to his hope that Christ will heal. Even if Jesus seems to demur, this father will not abandon his quest or his confidence. He is not disappointed.

Jesus grants the man's request—well, He grants most of it: "Go; your son will live" (John 4:50). The man had hoped that Jesus would travel with him to Capernaum, where his son lay dying. Jesus decides not to go, but with His response, He gives the man what he most desires and evokes from him what he most needs. Jesus' words to the official—actually, not only the words, but the very person and being of Jesus Himself—cultivate in the man a new certainty, a new confidence, a new trust, and a new faith.

Maybe when he left Capernaum, the official had been the sort of signs-and-wonders believer that Jesus decries. As we know, Capernaum had experienced its share of Jesus' miracles. Ample empirical evidence was available to support a signs-and-wonders faith in the miracle-working Prophet from Nazareth. The faith that brought the official to Jesus may have been shallow and poorly founded, but it was faith enough to warrant a trip to Cana.

But now that the official had come face-to-face with Jesus, now that he had made his request, now that Jesus had forced him to go deeper in faith with that provocative response, now that Jesus had promised the desire of the father's heart—now, the official grasps the reality of faith. Better, the reality of faith grasps him. It is all about Jesus. The official believes.

It is stated with disarming simplicity, but is wonderfully profound: "The man believed the word that Jesus spoke to him and went on his way" (John 4:50). Jesus' word was all the man needed—at least now, that was all he needed. Jesus did not need to accompany him back to Capernaum. Jesus did not need to see his son. Jesus did not need to touch his son. Jesus only needed to say the word; that was enough. He didn't even need to say it twice or seek to reassure the man.

It is significant that John uses a potent (*the* most potent) word for *believe*. The word for "to believe" is the same one that is typically translated "to have faith in." It is actually the verb form of the Greek noun for faith, *pistis*. John is not saying that the father merely decided to "go along with it for lack of any better option," "take Jesus' word for it," or "give Jesus the benefit of the doubt" (like you do when the mechanic assures you that you need new front struts). John is telling us that this man has already parted company with his contemporaries. He is not like them. The people are preoccupied with a signs-and-wonders sort of faith—but not this man. His faith does not need signs and wonders. All he needs now is the word of Jesus. Signs and wonders are not required. He has a faith that is content to cling to a word of Jesus. The promise of Jesus is sufficient.

We aren't told how far the official had to travel before the conviction of his faith was confirmed by the report of his slaves. If the slaves left with their news as soon as the official's son was up and about—and if the motivation of their good news spurred their pace as much as it spurred the haste of the father to return home to his son—the happy meeting would have been at the halfway mark. The official is out of sight of his son and out of sight of Jesus, but he does not need the affirmation of sight. He has the word of Jesus.

A quick check of the facts confirms what he already knows: his son was healed at the exact moment Jesus had said the word. And then, John confirms what we already know: "And he himself believed" (John 4:53). Of course, he did. He had believed the word of Jesus about his son, and now he believes in Jesus. This is the real climax of the story. The boy's healing had been a foregone conclusion—of course, he would be healed. What remained to be seen was the response of the father. But Jesus wins this challenge as well. Faith in signs and wonders has been replaced with faith in Jesus.

And then John adds a wonderful detail to verse 53: "and all his household." The man, his wife, his son, his slaves, and anyone else who lived under his roof all believed in Jesus. This is the great victory of this story and the reason John counts this as the second sign of his Gospel. A dying boy healed from a distance at the mere word of Jesus is a great feat and counts as a miracle, that's true. But the miracle that matters and holds the attention of John is the outcome—the official believes, and his whole household believes. That is the miracle.

Jumping two thousand years from the time of Christ and the official to our own day is a challenging enterprise. Their world was unlike ours in so many ways. But people remain the same in every age, and we can draw some important applications from this story of the official whose greatest legacy is his success as an exemplary father. Jesus chided the official's contemporaries for a faith founded only on signs and wonders. The relative scarcity of signs and wonders in our daily lives might suggest that this criticism holds no relevance for us. And it is true; it is not the preponderance of remarkable miracles that grounds our faith. Still, we do struggle, with a tendency to overestimate the importance of empirical evidence as normative for matters as important as faith. That people experience debilitating angst when empirical evidence is offered to refute some tenet of faith reflects the enduring propensity of people to put more trust in what can be measured and scientifically verified than in a simple word of God that can only be grasped by faith. Simply taking Jesus at His word proves as great a challenge for us as it did for the official.

While Jesus rightly commands the place of prominence in every Gospel account, our interest in fathers naturally compels us to think a bit more about the father in our story. We don't know much, but we know enough to recognize him as a remarkable man. All that we said about Jairus and the importance of humility before Christ applies again in this narrative. The official understands his position and his dependence on Jesus—hence the resultant faith worked by God. But the nameless official earns our admiration and our careful consideration in particular by his impressive impact on his family. Face-to-face with the Savior, the official learned the wonder of faith that simply trusts. He then transmitted this same faith to those in his family. Perhaps the father told them what Jesus said, or perhaps they heard the Gospel from others—maybe even from Jesus Himself on another occasion.

The official was a man who left a mark on his family. Not a mark of sin, shame, and suffering, the kind of mark we have come to expect of too many failed fathers, but a mark of joy, integrity, and faith. The more cynical might contend that the official's household joined their *pater familias*, their father/lord of the family, in his new faith only by obligation. It is true that throughout most of history, the ruler of a domain, be it a family or a state, typically determined the faith of its subjects. The cherished idol of individual sovereignty regnant in our culture had yet to make its spectacular entrance on the world stage. But it was something more than mere respect for authority that led everyone in the household to the certainty of faith in Christ. It may have been something the man himself said that he heard from Jesus.

We know it is unwise to argue a point not present in the text itself. What combination of forces was at work in shaping the thinking and the faith of the royal official's household we cannot say with certainty. But, with the conviction of certainty and without any speculation, we can say much about a father's influence on twenty-first-century families. Most Christian fathers have been told—probably told more times than they care to recall—that they are responsible for the spiritual care of their family. They have been told this because it is true. Exactly what this means in practice, though, is often far from clear. Aware of an unsettling but vague burden of responsibility for their families' spiritual well-being, most fathers have no idea what to do about it—other than to have family devotions, another thing they have been told more times than they care to recall. But even if he does manage to establish the practice a few days a week, reading a 90-second devotion with attached prayer at the end of breakfast hardly constitutes the fulfillment of a father's spiritual responsibility for his family. Devotions are a good idea, but not a panacea.

The reality of a father's role and responsibility in the care of his family is neither as confounding nor as contrived as often portrayed. There are no formulas, no secrets, and no insightful books to read. There is, instead, the incalculable force of a life of faith and character consistently lived. When children can watch their father live what he declares; when they can see continuity between the personal choices he makes and the expectations he has of others; when they see harmony between his commitment to Sunday worship and the way he spends his leisure; in short, when children see in their father integrity, not only will they love him, but they will respect, honor, and emulate him. In a sense, being a father who makes an impact of blessing on his family is less about doing and more about being. And that's what makes fatherhood at once disarmingly more simple and vastly more challenging than most men understand.

At the heart of such a man of integrity is the vital core of faith merely received—the kind of faith discovered by the official, the kind of faith made possible by the word and work of Jesus. Faithful fathers are all the same that way—they all live as the official learned to live, with Christ and His example at the center of life. Men like this always make an impact.

## Questions

1. It has become axiomatic that most men would sooner lose a limb than stop and ask for directions. Assuming this is true (which is debatable), why might this be the case?

2. Read John 4:46–47. What character traits or virtues might be suggested by the behavior of the royal official from Capernaum as described in these verses?

3. Read John 4:48–51. What is your reaction to Jesus' first words? Without claiming to know God's mind, what purpose does Jesus seem to have in this response?

4. In Greek, the word for the polite address "Sir" is the same as the cry of faith "Lord!" Either one is *kyrie*. Which way do you think it should be translated in verse 49?

5. What led the official to expect that Jesus would come with him to lay hands on his son? Why do you think Jesus chose to heal this man's son with only a distant word?

6. Read John 4:52–54. The official learned to trust Jesus' word more than he trusted the evidence of his own senses. How does this truth apply to the interface between the data of science and reason and the convictions of faith?

7. What factors do you think precipitated the conversion of the official's entire household? Why is this the climax of the story?

8. From your own experience, what sort of influence does a father have on the spiritual health of his family? What is the most important thing a man can do as a positive spiritual influence on his family?

9. What is the relation between faith (which God works) and faithfulness (which is a father's responsibility)?

10. Some Bible translations suggest that the official is a "royal" official. Presuming those translations are accurate, how does 1 Peter 2:9 suggest another way of reading this title? What wider application might this title have?

# The Prodigal's Father

Who is this father? What kind of man does the things this father does? What kind of father handles his children the way this father handles his sons? For that matter, what kind of father raised sons to be so glaringly deficient in the most basic expectations of behavior? Who is this father? This is the father of the prodigal son.

One liability of a comfortable familiarity with the stories recorded in the Bible is that we can lose sight of important peculiarities of those stories. The story of the lost son is certainly among the most cherished, most familiar, and most unusual of the Bible. We commonly know it as the parable of the prodigal or wasteful son, but it could as easily have been the tale of the careless, licentious, disrespectful, rebellious, self-indulgent, puerile, insensitive, or stupid son. Take your pick; the son at the center of the story satisfies every adjective in the list. But this is not the peculiarity we are prone to ignore—the sort of son Jesus describes is familiar to us all. There's nothing odd about the son. It is the father who is extraordinary.

Jesus' great parable is the third in a series prompted by fresh criticism of His disreputable company—"tax collectors and sinners" (Luke 15:1). First, we meet a shepherd who leaves ninety-nine sheep to find one. Then, we are introduced to a woman with a similar obsession for a lost coin. By intention, we are led to identify with the shepherd and the woman. Their actions are expected and understandable. "What man of you . . . what woman," Jesus asks, would fail to do the same? Naturally, people search to find things that are precious to them—we would all do the same. But the third story has no introduction and no immediate identification between the reader and the father who has lost his son. This father does things that are not expected. He does things that are not even reasonable.

The extraordinary, even rash, behavior of this fictive father is immediately apparent. The younger son's request for his share of the inheritance is not normal or acceptable. He's not looking for a cash advance or a little help from his father. Impatient for what presumably he would inherit only after his father's death, this impertinent son wants it all—now. The wealth is his father's. The son has no right to it, at least not yet, and the father gives it to him, which is unreal. This action is even more fantastic than the request of the son. What man would do such a thing? An absurd request like this should at least prompt a conversation. But, even if it did, this father's talk with his son could only develop like this: "What do you need the money for?" "Oh, I don't know. I just want to spend it." "Hmm . . . Okay, here you go. Take it all."

That is crazy. Maybe the father would give him a little—a test to see how things went. Even better, after learning the son's investment strategy, an intense time of training in responsibility and financial management would be implemented before the boy saw a penny. Best of all, the father would explore what would possess his own son to make such a painful, disrespectful request and then address the root issue. But this father does what no father should do. He hands over the money as though he had already died.

Enabling the realization of his son's ultimate fantasy debauch is only the beginning of the father's inexplicable behavior. The son leaves home, and the father watches him go. The man was capable of a reasoned conversation—he had one later, with his older son— but there is no conversation recorded as this son sets off. Perhaps the household is not exactly sad to see him go. The prolonged party runs its course, and repentance eventually claims the boy, but no one back home knows it. But it doesn't matter what they know. As soon as the father catches sight of the shadow that is his rebellious son, he flies to the boy, embraces him in his arms, and kisses him. He doesn't wait to hear what this insolent son has to say.

When the penitent is able to deliver his well-rehearsed speech, the father achieves new extremes of incredible deeds. There is no discussion about broken responsibility or the need to reestablish shattered trust. There is no negotiation about how things will work in the near-term to make sure that the son is ready to resume his place in the family. There is no tough love carefully crafted to bring the son to greater maturity and character. There is none of that. There is only immediate restoration to his privileged place and a party—a party for the party child.

The disgust of the boy's big brother should surprise no one. The mystery is why he was left in the fields while the rest of the household embarked on the celebration of the decade. A servant has to fill him in on the big news. At minimum, wisdom would suggest that the father should have orchestrated a family meeting with the older brother included—he had also paid a price for his little brother's antics.

There is nothing normal about any of this. There is nothing normal about this father. And it's all just fine, because it's this way by design. This is Jesus' parable, and it is making precisely the point He wants to make. The peculiarities of the parable, and especially of the father, don't detract from the story—they make the story. It is neither impious nor profane to call attention to the obvious absurdities of this fictional family of three. The abnormality of this father is the essential, disarming beauty implicit in this outstanding story. The father is not typical. He is not predictable. He is not regular or ordinary. He defies all expectations and does what no human father could be expected to do. This father is, of course, the Father. That's the point.

An old rule of thumb is that parables must not be interpreted allegorically. Actually, this is a good rule to follow when interpreting any part of Scripture. Unless the text spells them out, one shouldn't look for neat correspondences between the characters or events of a story and people and events in contemporary life. The practice of allegorizing reads too much into texts and causes one to overlook what the text does say and do. This is clearly the case with the story of the lost son. If we read this parable in order to mine the details, establish parallels, and generate principles, we are following the path of allegory. The popularity of this path with this parable does nothing to salvage the method. The parable of the lost son is told for one reason. It is not a treasure trove of biblical principles for successful parenting. Regardless of the similarities and ease of application, it is not an allegory of the modern family complete with inept, indulgent fathers, rebellious boys, and self-righteous sons. So we must resist the allegorizing impulse.

In fact, we must resist even the temptation to read the story as a guide to Christian parenting. This is another common move: if the father in the story is the Father, then surely he must set the standard for good parenting. But the parable of the prodigal is certainly not a place a father should turn for solid parenting advice. The story has a different purpose than to offer a case study in effective fatherhood. The actions and inactions of the father in the opening scenes of the parable are not intended to be normative or even exemplary. They are there for only one purpose: to quickly set the stage for the important action that follows. To be found, the son must be lost. The action that matters, the point of this story, is the father's reception of the lost son. This father does one thing well—but this one thing is so enormously important and so exceedingly valuable that it rightly obscures every other aspect of the story. Like the other two "lost parables," this parable is the proclamation of the Gospel. That's the only purpose.

Okay, it's also a rather pointed call for the scribes, Pharisees, and other religious snobs to repent and receive grace themselves, but even that serves the main point of the Gospel. In fact, the older, better son actually makes the point even more explicitly. The younger son was obviously lost and needed—but never expected—what only the father could give. The older son was every bit as lost, only his crying need was not as apparent and was only manifest in the light of the grace given to his brother.

Faithful and obedient, his self-righteousness mushroomed into rejection of his father and his father's grace. Nevertheless, he lived still in desperate need of his father's grace—and he had it, though he failed to recognize it. The father's appeal to this son is the appeal of love—the same love showered on the younger brother. The story ends with the Gospel call extended again, and the final result is unknown. But the story is not about the sons. It is about the father—it is about the father's spectacular capacity to forgive and to celebrate the return, the resurrection, the salvation of the lost.

This father, then, is absolutely nothing like any we have encountered. Unlike any of the previous fathers considered in this study, this father does not offer us insights into the task of fatherhood or principles for powerful parenting. He does not provide a paradigm for great fatherhood. He gives us something far more important. He gives us the Gospel. Yes, of course, the father of the prodigal calls us to love our own children with the delivery of the Gospel. When sons or daughters timidly creep into your presence to plead forgiveness, give it—effusively and liberally, give it. The parable does give us that mandate. But the core of the story, and the point of this father, is that this Gospel, this uncalculated, unstinted, unbelievable Gospel, is for you.

Of course, this is the right, really the only, place to conclude a study on courageous fathers. The unhappy reality is that one cannot contemplate the task of fatherhood and the demands of this sacred trust without enduring a hefty dose of debilitating unease, regret, and guilt. This is not a comfortable business. The expectations are so exacting, the responsibilities so unrelenting, the burden so uncompromising that no father can escape the call of biblical fatherhood unscathed, with a light and carefree heart. Every man falls short. Every man fails. Every father needs what the Father gives, including you. You need the unhesitating embrace. You need the exultant reception. You need the unrestrained celebration. You need the Gospel. And you get it.

God meets your need for the Gospel in ways that are every bit as tangible and certain as they were for the repentant prodigal. That boy knew he was forgiven—he felt his father's arms around him, he heard the orders given to kill the fatted calf, he saw the ring on his finger. It was all very real. God the Father continues to deliver His Gospel to His children in ways that can't be missed. That's the purpose of the Church. When the pastor preaches that your sins are forgiven through Jesus Christ, it is the Father who is speaking. When your friend assures you of God's good plans for your life, it is the comfort of the Father that you experience. When your mother held you close and told you she forgave you, it was the peace of the Father that was being delivered to you. When you hear the Word and receive the Sacraments, it is the forgiveness of the Father that the Son, your Brother, shares with you. Forgiveness is located. God gives it through His Church. God gives it through His pastor. God gives it through His people. And you receive that grace and the Father's forgiveness just as the sons of the parable received it.

So live in that reality. Live confidently today, knowing God has graced you with His unrestrained, unbounded forgiveness. Live knowing God loves you with the kind of love that the father had for his sons—a love that does not calculate, a love that does not make demands, a love that does not make sense. God has that kind of love for you. You have that kind of Father. It is the great certainty that undergirds every part of your life, and it does not change. God finds and claims what is lost. He finds you and claims you. It is your story. The Father with the fantastic love is your Father. The Father who is always ready to forgive is your Father. This truth does not change with circumstances and is not dependent on your performance. Regardless of how you've done in the past with your responsibilities, regardless of how you are doing in the present or will do in the future, the truth of God's unfathomable love and incredible capacity to forgive remains constant. This is the great truth of the Gospel. This is the great truth of the parable of the lost son. It is the central truth of your life.

Clearly, this is a truth that deserves to be passed along to others. Make sure you start with your own sons and daughters. By example and by word, bring your children to know and to delight in the same Gospel of God that defines your life. Bring those children entrusted to you to the font to be claimed by God. Tell them the stories of God's love and plans for His people. Teach them to kneel to receive grace they can never deserve. Nurture in them the joy of the forgiveness of their sins. This is the great message of the prodigal's father.

The Gospel does not trump the tasks of fatherhood. Never in competition, but always in concert with the continuous declaration and celebration of the Father's forgiveness, you exert yourself with unflagging zeal to the fulfillment of the responsibility you have been given. You strive to be the best father, the best husband, the best employee, the best man you can be. The Gospel is the dynamic reality that animates the life of God's people. Living in the forgiveness of the Gospel, you delight to do what God has given you to do. There are people depending on you to do it. That's why the parable of the prodigal does not reduce to a series of principles for successful parenting. That misses the point. Use it that way, and you end up a failed, permissive parent passing out a senti-mentalized, eviscerated Gospel without significance. Living the parable of the prodigal does not mean always telling your kids yes, never holding them accountable for their actions, and ignoring the reality of choices poorly made. It means being a father who knows the grace of the Gospel, shares the grace of the Gospel, and then strives with all of his energy to fulfill his responsibilities by teaching his children to do the same.

Two great truths are at work at once in all of life. The man of God who is committed to God's call lives both truths: with unrelenting effort he strives to be a good man, and with humility and relief he succumbs to the unmerited grace that God gives. This is the Christian life. The Bible, of course, presents both truths. From what God commands, and from fathers of the Bible, we learn what God expects. Here, in the Gospel of Luke, though, we are not given one more father with one more lesson to teach. Here we learn, here we experience, the most beautiful reality of all—the message of the son lost and found again. This concluding story, this final father, does not present the ultimate example to emulate; this last story provides a Father who forgives and loves you! This is not a Father with standards to which you aspire, but a Father with grace to which you surrender. This is your Father.

## Questions

1. Think of a time or two when you were in need of forgiveness. As appropriate, share with the group. What makes the experience of being forgiven so memorable?

2. Read Luke 15:11–21. When the son comes to his senses (v. 17), is this the same thing as repenting? What brought about the change?

3. Why might the rule about only one point of application be particularly apt in the case of the parable of the lost son? How might this parable be misused?

4. Read Luke 15:22–32. Offering reasons for your choice, with which character do you most closely identify? What makes this family and its dynamics seem unreal, and on the other hand, ring with authenticity?

5. How might it be argued that both sons in the story were lost? What did the father do to extend grace to each? Why was his approach to each son different?

6. In what sense is grace always at least somewhat bizarre and illogical? How does this help account for people's rejection of God's grace?

7. Why is it important to read the parable not as a lesson, but as a gift?

8. Where can a father turn to find the comfort of the Gospel and guidance for his task?

9. How can delivering the message of the Gospel become an excuse for indulgent, permissive, or just plain lazy parenting? How does a father extend the Gospel of the lost son to his own children without forsaking his responsibility to guide, protect, and correct?

10. What one truth from this study will find a place in the way you live in the days ahead?

# Small Group Leader Guide

This guide will help guide you discover the truths of God's Word. It is not, however, exhaustive, nor is it designed to be read aloud during your session.

1. Before you begin, spend some time in prayer, asking God to strengthen your faith through a study of His Word. The Scriptures were written so that we might believe in Jesus Christ and have life in His name (John 20:31). Also, pray for participants by name.

2. Before your meeting, review the session material, read the Bible passages, and answer the questions in the spaces provided. Your familiarity with the session will give you confidence as you lead the group.

3. As a courtesy to others, begin and end each session on time.

4. Have a Bible dictionary or similar resource handy to look up difficult or unfamiliar names, words, and places. Ask participants to help you in this task. Be sure that each participant has a Bible and a study guide.

5. Ask for volunteers to read introductory paragraphs and Bible passages. A simple "Thank you" will encourage them to volunteer again.

6. See your role as a conversation facilitator rather than a lecturer. Don't be afraid to give participants time to answer questions. By name, thank each participant who answers; then invite other input. For example, you might say, "Thank you, Al. Would anyone else like to share?"

7. Now and then, summarize aloud what the group has learned by studying God's Word.

8. Remember that the questions provided are discussion starters. Allow participants to ask questions that relate to the session. However, keep discussions on track with the session.

9. Everyone is a learner! If you don't know the answer to a question, simply tell participants that you need time to look at more Scripture passages or to ask your pastor.

# Adam

1. In his Genesis commentary, Martin Luther wrote about Adam with glowing admiration, as a virtual superman who possessed the height of human potential physically, intellectually, and spiritually. Perhaps Adam can be rightly thought of in this way. It is just as likely, though, that thinking of Adam conjures visions of the first couple being driven out of the garden in shame and disgrace. It must also be admitted that Adam's performance when confronted by God after the fall is less than exemplary—passing the buck by blaming Eve is hardly what we would expect from a chivalrous, stand-up guy! Adam is the father of man, but also the father of sin. His legacy is ambiguous at best.

2. Answers will depend on the interests and ideas of those present. While speculation is ultimately just that—speculation—the value in thinking about the unknown details is that it encourages participants to consider the full humanity of Adam as an individual man, husband, and father. It is helpful to remember that Adam—and every biblical character—felt real emotions, experienced relational strife and joy, and reacted uniquely to all of these things just like men do today.

3. Obviously, Abel does not count—he's dead. Without a wife or heirs, Abel is of no account to the subsequent story of God's people. The same with Cain. While Cain secures a wife and sires progeny, they do not figure into the story of God's interactions with His people. Cain has set himself against the will of God, and his descendants are not numbered among the descendants of Adam (detailed in ch. 5). By defying God's will, Cain has cut himself out of the plan.

4. The text, Genesis 5:3, credits Seth with having the image and likeness of Adam. The same is not said of Cain or Abel (Genesis 4:1–2). This is likely because the thread of man's history will follow the line of Seth, and so it is stressed that Adam's descendants bear the image given to Adam at his creation. Still, it is

arguable that Adam's defiance of his Creator is best exemplified in his firstborn son who takes the place of God and chooses to become the lord of life and death.

5. The point of the commission is that it is a commission—it still stands. The directive given to Adam was still in place even after the fall and its consequent curses. Adam fulfilled what he had been given to do—in spite of the fact that he had destroyed the beauty of what God had originally created and intended. So Adam lived, as we live, in the tension between the command and promise of God and the resultant brokenness of the creation and the strains in relationships. That Adam trusted God's command and promise even after the fall indicates Adam's faith and is unquestionably a significant demonstration of courage. Adam's willingness to become a father is itself a remarkable statement of obedience to God and confidence in God's provision.

6. There will certainly be overlap in the answers that are suggested, but each man should be able to recognize the particular responsibilities that he has to serve those members of the creation that are around him—especially those who rely on him in special ways, such as wife and children. The point is to learn to see the various tasks that make up life in the context of God's plan and God's arrangement for His creation—an arrangement that forces us to live in interdependence.

7. The narrative suggests several possible distractions including hobbies and career. Most importantly, though, might be the individualism and entitlement attitudes that permeate so much of Western culture. The pursuit of individual fulfillment leaves little time or energy for the pursuit of someone else's agenda, so the needs of that someone can seem like a burdensome imposition, even if that someone is your own child.

8. Given the pressures and assumptions of the world around us, a man's determination to serve his wife and children so that they know and follow Christ can only be achieved with God's grace and strength. Living with the vocation of father foremost in a man's thinking will put him at odds with the rest of the world and its agenda. Perhaps the greatest battle to be fought will not be with others who challenge his choices, but with himself and his own sinful desires to demand his own agenda and satisfy his own aspirations. Of course, ideally, as a man grows in conformity with Christ, his own desire will be to be the best father that he can be.

9. In His mercy, God fills our lives with many joys—even when the routine of that life and the vocational demands of that life are sometimes hard, inglorious, unrecognized, and unappreciated. That God speaks the promise of a Savior to Adam is Gospel, indeed. Adam is not left in his failure and ruin. God will make things right. The promise was one that would require much patient waiting on the part of Adam's descendants, but it was kept. God's promises always are. So it is with the work of fatherhood. Much is expected and much is promised. Regardless of your struggles with keeping fatherhood in its rightful, primary spot, God speaks grace and forgiveness to you for the sake of the new Adam who puts everything back in its right place (Romans 5:12–21).

10. Participants should be challenged to identify one idea or lesson that will make a tangible difference in the way they live in the immediate future. How those ideas might be put into concrete action would be a worthy discussion for the group.

# Noah

1. Obviously, this question is intended as little more than a question to prime discussion. Given the absence of any clear direction from the text, all ideas are equally possible . . . or impossible. (In other words, don't twist this into a serious and dogmatic discussion!)

2. Several themes present themselves. Noteworthy is the marked contrast between Noah and the rest of mankind. This is self-explanatory. What is less clear is the regret of God. How an omnipotent God can regret a choice is a bit of a puzzle. Without delving too deeply into questions of human responsibility and divine foreordination, it is clear what people do or fail to do impacts what God does. Perhaps it can be understood as God entering into time with His creatures and holding them accountable even as He continues to direct all things above and beyond all time and human action. Also of note is God's detailed and careful provision for Noah and his living cargo.

3. In light of the usual depictions of Noah and his neighbors, it is surprising that the text does not provide any hint of debauchery or sexual indulgence being the precipitating cause of God's wrath. Rather, the problem is violence—man rising up to assert himself against his neighbor. Violence might be common and numbing in our world, but from God's perspective it is a great evil. Violence is man taking the reins from God and doing what only God and His designees have the prerogative to do.

4. Implicit in the teaching of this lesson is Luther's foundational understanding of the two kinds of righteousness (AE 26:4–12). There is a righteousness of this world for which we humans are held accountable. But this righteousness does not save us from eternal death and hell, and cannot aid us one whit toward that salvation. We are responsible to be good people, and by so living, we can achieve a level of righteousness. Along with this, there is an altogether different kind of righteousness before God. This is

righteousness that God simply gives for the sake of Christ. This righteousness, and this righteousness alone, saves us from eternal death and hell. Luther calls the first *active righteousness* (we actively do it) and the second *passive righteousness*. Keeping these two kinds of righteousness straight is vital not only for this story, but for all scriptural narratives.

5. Righteousness before God is passive. This means that man does nothing. Just to be clear—man does *nothing*. To say that God does it all and that man lives in this righteousness by being thoroughly and abjectly dependent on God paints man in rather a pathetic light, to say the least. Fallen man, whether simple and violent or sophisticated and proud, refuses to accept such a demeaning and humbling portrait, and so rejects the idea of grace. When man will not admit his absolute dependence on God, then grace cannot be present. To clarify and reinforce this point, check out the explanation to the Third Article of the Apostles' Creed in Luther's Small Catechism.

6. This is not one of the happy moments in the Noah narrative. But, in typical biblical bluntness, it is told without any attempt to varnish or spin the facts. Noah's actions are inexplicable. We are given no hint about why it happened. Perhaps it is best not to know. The mere fact that sin happens should cause us all to live both kindly toward those in sin and circumspectly lest we inadvertently follow them. The same holds true for Ham's despicable behavior in stark contrast to the honor and humility demonstrated by Shem and Japheth. There simply is no accounting for man's proclivity to sin. Why Ham failed to incorporate the lessons of his father is a mystery without certain resolution. Speculating about the "why" simply makes the shock of sin a little easier to bear, but also serves to numb one to the deadly threat sin poses to us all.

7. There are many ways to approach this question. To start, teaching a child to have faith—or perhaps better said, *instilling* faith in a child—is by far the most important task of a father. Yet, the investment of too many Christian fathers toward achieving this goal pales in comparison to the investment they make in their child's ability to block a shot on goal. Also of interest is the fact that even the best work of a father can result in a Ham who goes his own way and rejects what his father worked to instill. On top of all

this is the realization that faith is the work of no man, but only and always the exclusive work of the Holy Spirit.

8. The group should be able to offer a multitude of good thoughts, hopefully based on personal experience. The list should be sure to include the example that a man sets by his consistent living—exemplified in Noah—striving to fulfill his duty, but relying fully on God. Integrity between a Sunday confession and Monday living is another key ingredient in successful Christian parenting.

9. The flood had destroyed all life outside the ark, but it had not altered God's plan or purposes for man. The first Great Commission stood, and Noah and his descendants did not need to wonder about their purpose in the world. They were still to preside over the creation (v. 2) and be busy filling the earth (v. 1 and 7). The rainbow and its covenant were a brilliant reminder of God's place in man's life and man's dependence on his Creator. Man could only trust the promise and cling to what God had declared: the forces of nature that would never submit to man's will would never operate outside the restraining and marvelously loving will of God.

10. For the man who is willing to see them, God supplies many reminders of His provision and of our position of dependence on His care and mercy toward us. Even morning aches and pains serve as sharp reminders of our finitude. The incomparable beauty of a fruit tree can remind us of a God who continues to give all that we need, as well as the delight generated by a creature doing what it was created to do.

# Abraham

1. Don't expect uniformity on this question! Take note of those in the group who did not experience Sunday School. What can the varying experiences of different participants teach the group?

2. Trivial though it may seem, Sunday School singing does play a role in the formation of faith. Children form ideas about God and His Church through these harmless songs. Those responsible for such singing should carefully consider exactly *what* is being communicated (intentionally or not) by the singing of any given song. Does it convey truth about God? Does it portray God as distant or indifferent? Does it edify those who sing it to be strong in faith? Does it unnecessarily trivialize what is holy? Of course, having fun in church is also a very good thing, and somber and severe demeanors or singing is hardly the goal!

3. While we are not privy to all the motivations and thoughts of Abraham, this may well be a simple matter of preferring a sure thing to a mere hope. Abraham already had a son on the verge of manhood; why not expect the fulfillment of the promise through that son? This demonstrates the loyalty of Abraham to Ishmael, but also may indicate weariness with waiting!

4. Abraham's concern for the son he was already raising indicates the sort of love and loyalty a father would have toward his son—even if the son is not (for reasons that are never revealed) God's heir of choice. While it might seem commendable for a father to set no limit on paternal loyalty, God's Word must always guide the extent of this loyalty. Indeed, the height of loyalty and love toward a child is to hold that child within God's will—though this may not be particularly pleasant.

5. This question is intended to help the participants consider the reality of the challenge that confronted Abraham. It is likely that many of those in the group will be able to recall situations they have experienced (or heard of) when a father was compelled to follow a demanding and even painful path for the sake of

obeying the will of God for his child. That God's will may not always coincide with human logic or reason should not be too surprising. God is not subject to the dictates of human rationality. Of course, in the big picture, a commitment to conform to God's will is always the most reasonable and successful course for one of God's creatures.

6. This is a perennial question among people who are serious about living as Christian disciples. The answer is not as complicated as most assume. God's Law, wired into the creation (natural law) and specifically revealed in His Word is His will for His creatures. When any given course of action is being considered, the criteria is simple—does the planned choice conform to the Law of God? Obviously, within God's will there is considerable latitude for a variety of decisions. If a number of choices seem to fit within the parameters of the Law, then human reason, wise counsel, and even personal preferences are legitimate factors to help in reaching a decision.

7. Given the culture in which we live and the preference for the individual over the community, it is not too surprising that people would consider the facts about Jesus' sacrifice and death and conclude that it adds up to child abuse. It is worth noting that such an assertion is quite helpful if one is trying to deflect the claims of God. If God is guilty of child abuse, then the cross may be dismissed and its declaration of my own personal guilt and responsibility may be ignored. A critical idea to counter this charge is to reassert the place of creature in submission to Creator—God does not submit to human reason and standards of justice. One should also recall that the sacrificial plan of redemption originated also with the Son—it was love alone that drove Him as well. Jesus willingly laid down His life for us—and took it up again (John 10:17–18).

8. Obviously, the idea is to draw more closely the connection between the story of Isaac and Christ's Calvary sacrifice. The substitution of a ram for the young Isaac is the heart of what is called the vicarious atonement—the understanding that at the cross Jesus paid the price for sinful men. He was the substitute, or vicar, for those who deserved to die for their sin. At Mount Moriah, then, we have a wonderful foreshadowing of that vicarious substitution, as a ram becomes the sacrifice in place of Isaac. The ram of God saves Isaac, and the Ram of God, Jesus, saves us by paying the price in our place.

9. No human is able to create or sustain faith. This is work that only God can do. A father, then, lives under no illusions. He cannot make his children have faith. Only God, the Holy Spirit, authors faith in a person. Yet, the Holy Spirit has promised clearly to work through His chosen means—through Word and Sacrament. When these are absent, the Spirit does not work. Additionally, human responsibility is not negated by stressing divine activity. God converts, but humans must speak the Gospel, administer the Sacrament, and strive to live consistently with that confession. The Holy Spirit calls people to faith, but human sin and failure to fulfill God's will can thwart God's plan and prevent faith.

10. Faith is always demonstrated in action; James makes this clear in his (in)famous reference to Abraham being justified by works (James 2:21–24). Justified by faith alone, faith is never alone, Luther reminds us, and so we find ways to live out the reality of justification. Whether learning to wait, or obey, or trust God's course, help group members consider the challenges and opportunities they will encounter as they seek to incorporate lessons learned from Father Abraham into their daily living.

# Isaac

1. Given the abundance of unique names in fashion, participants should have little trouble offering many suggestions. Personal accounts of significant names will vary widely. Some will relate tales of generations-old family names; others may have an interesting account of creative or meaningful naming on the part of their parents; many will have no story at all.

2. Though the text does not specifically record it, it is impossible to believe that both of the events were not significant occurrences in the life of Isaac. They would have left an indelible impression upon his character. While it is speculation, it is not hard to imagine Isaac gaining valuable experience about the lengths one must sometimes go to follow God's will. Since this is speculation, the possible lessons learned are virtually limitless, but would include trusting God's provision, obedience without limit, the worth of a worthy spouse, an appreciation for the spouse he gained, a commitment not to squander a heritage so carefully and daringly preserved, and perhaps even a certain wariness about the region of Mount Moriah.

3. Participants may be slow to divulge such personal information, so if the leader has one or two things in mind he is willing to relate, it might help prime the group. It is worth noting that these formative events need not be dramatic or sensational. It is often the routine and repetitious events from ordinary life that have the most formative power in our lives. The point is to help those in the group to recognize the impact of life events on their own thinking and character. Awareness of this reality could prove a powerful tool to more effective parenting.

4. Some in the group might think it odd that King Abimelech and the rest of the Philistines were so accommodating to Isaac after his "she's my sister" game. It might also be considered a bit strange that Isaac reacted with such equanimity to the unprovoked harassment of the Philistines. The fact that Isaac did not retaliate

or demand his rights could be attributed merely to his desire to be a gracious guest in a foreign land. Or, more significantly, it might reflect his commitment to trust God for His provision and to rely on the power of deference and humility rather than bravado and belligerence to solve his difficulties.

5. As a rule, the Proverb about the force of a "soft answer" (Proverbs 15:1) is given far too little credence by most men. Within the unguarded atmosphere of domestic life, it is particularly easy and common for men to deal with challenges and affronts with a volley of high-volume words, rather than exercising the wisdom of deference and humility that refuses to stand on its own rights and instead yields from strength. The impact of such an approach in the home could be quite profound and transformative. Of course, the text also contains many other potential lessons.

6. The term *dysfunction* seems to fit the circumstances pretty accurately. However, it is possible that in an otherwise healthy family, this event was an anomaly driven by Rebekah's memory of God's word to her when the twins were still *in utero.* Regardless of one's explanation, it is intriguing to see how God uses human actions and choices—even sinful ones—to further His plan. Jacob would be blessed. The covenant would move forward through his line. It was all happening just as God had designed it to happen. God's plan does not depend on human virtue or success.

7. We are not all called to headline-grabbing roles within God's plan. Isaac is a wonderful scriptural example of a man who lived faithfully doing what he had been given to do, even if that was as simple as raising Jacob to be another faithful generation of God's covenant people. There is no trivial or insignificant task if God gives it. Isaac reminds us of the beauty of ordinary life lived within God's purposes—precisely the kind of life that many of us live. That ordinary Isaac still has his place among the patriarchs is affirmation of the importance of ordinary saints.

8. It seems Rebekah hatches the plot in an effort to protect Jacob, and involves Isaac for the sake of official paternal sanction. Whether this is an example of the wife planting an idea, or actually directing affairs, or simply Isaac and Rebekah in agreement on the right course for Jacob, is not clear from the text. While we are perhaps more inclined to skepticism, it is entirely possible that Isaac reached a conclusion similar to Rebekah's regarding Jacob's

future. Regardless of the originator of the idea, Isaac owned it and directly intervened for the sake of his son.

9. Genesis 35:8 mentions the death of Rebekah's nurse, but the only other time Rebekah's name appears is to tell us that she was buried in the same place as Isaac (Genesis 49:31). One can readily appreciate how seeing Jacob complete with sons, daughters, servants, and herds would have been an extraordinary moment for old Isaac. Every dream and prayer was vividly accomplished before his own eyes. The promise was being fulfilled, and Isaac again had reason to laugh.

10. Who exactly is doing the laughing, and why, is not clear from the name. Abraham and Sarah laughed in disbelief, then in joy. Rebekah and Jacob laughed in mocking scorn (at least figuratively), but in the course of many years of family life, must also have laughed with Isaac on many occasions. Isaac himself had much to foster his own laughter. But it is God who laughs best, as His plan is advancing just as He intended (check out Psalm 2:4).

# Jacob

1. Most members of the group probably know someone who is from a big family (the term is intentionally left vague, but Jacob's twelve sons certainly qualify). It is interesting most people don't consider family size to be a subject that has anything to do with their relationship with God. It is the intent of this and the next question to challenge this assumption and suggest that the number of children in a family does hold a spiritual dimension that should not be ignored.

2. Notions about global overpopulation linger even in the Church's culture, and the standards of society have a way of dictating the choices of those in the Church, so that also among Christians the United States' average of 1.86 kids per family (US Census, 2000) seems normal—and having more kids may seem a bit odd. Arguments about desired standards of living, the ability to parent well, and consumption of resources are not irrelevant, but must be weighed with God's intentions for marriage and the stark reality that one of the most effective ways to grow the Church is through biological growth. To whom much is given, much is expected, and investment in future generations is a stellar place to invest resources.

3. In Exodus 20:5, which Luther included in his summary of the commandments, God declares that He is "a jealous God, visiting the iniquity of the fathers on the children to the third and fourth generation of those who hate Me." Experience often confirms the text as children replicate and exceed the vices of parents. Jacob offers proof of the idea, perfecting the lying and deception of father and grandfather. But Joseph seems to break the succession of dark inheritance. God's grace does make things new—even a family's spiritual and moral heritage.

4. Aided or even led by his mother, Jacob appears to act without a shred of hesitation or constraint. He puts on his best Esau costume, announces that he is Isaac's firstborn, invokes the

blessing of God to account for his speedy arrival, and confirms his deception with a second point-blank assertion of his identity as Esau. This is the depth of deceit. Given God's standards as recorded in Psalm 24, one would not be surprised by a divine visitation of wrath or at least rebuke. In fact, a well-placed lightning bolt would not much exceed (if at all) the expectations of justice.

5. Jacob's ladder is, for good reason, a much-loved section of Scripture. The bridge between heaven and earth is part of the fascination—but it is worth noting that the ladder is used by angels, and not by Jacob. More problematic is the context. What we expect from God is not what God does. There is no wrath, nor even a hint of rebuke. Instead there is blessing. Genesis 28:15 might provide the most help in sorting this out. God is the one who is acting. By His choice, He is going to use Jacob for His purpose—not the other way around. Jacob's evil will not thwart God's plan.

6. Even if one gives Laban his healthy share of the blame for rewarding Jacob's hard work with Leah, Jacob is certainly complicit in the sisters' maternal rivalry and desperate attempts to overcome one other. It is hard to know what to think about Leah and Rachel—both are sympathetic characters, but their solutions can hardly be considered God pleasing, as they violate God's plan for marriage as established at creation. It is easy to suggest wiser actions that Jacob might have taken. Still, in spite of this dysfunctional mess, God's purpose is advanced, and from four different mothers, Israel's twelve sons—and subsequent tribes—are born.

7. Read in the light of the preceding description of this event, one sees God's directing hand throughout this encounter and can, if so inclined, indulge in a little speculation about what God is trying to accomplish for Jacob. Jacob's literal wrestling with God is a microcosm of his life—struggling to reconcile his own designs and desires with God's overarching purposes. God wins, of course. Jacob becomes Israel. Those in the Church, God's new Israel, are not immune from similar struggles to obediently conform their lives to God's purposes.

8. While parents often make Herculean efforts at equity among their children, charges of favoritism are not uncommon and sometimes not ungrounded. Jacob's sad experience provides a stark reminder of what is at stake (Genesis 37). From their own experience, members of the group should be able to offer

suggestions about ways to recognize and celebrate the inherent differences among children without favoring one over another. As to what blinded Jacob, one can only speculate, but one could argue that a lifestyle of deception inevitably confounds one's powers of discretion.

9. Paul's whole point is that man does nothing to earn or ease God's giving of grace. Grace is unearned, period. God simply gives it without reason or logic to explain it. Jacob is loved for no apparent reason. That's what makes grace, grace. If Jacob had some redeeming character quality or attribute to impress God, or at least to catch His attention, then grace would disappear, obscured by the demands and expectations of the Law that Jacob had somehow fulfilled. If one must fulfill something before the divine blessings begin, then grace is destroyed, and Christianity collapses into just another moralism.

10. There is nothing simple about Jacob. One could easily conclude that he is a decidedly unlikable character; conversely, one could as easily realize that in Jacob we see a man not unlike most men—one who struggles to live rightly and who relies absolutely on grace. The long Jacob narrative in Genesis offers many lessons both positive and negative; the wise reader will be quick to incorporate at least some of those lessons into his own living.

# David

1. Odds are good that the challenge of Goliath will top the list of favorites, but there are other good candidates. This question is meant to refresh the memories of those in the group and provide a bit of a biographical overview of David. If participants have trouble getting beyond Goliath, it might be necessary to aid the discussion with some reminders: his anointing, soothing Saul with song, sparing Saul, winning Abigail, friendship with Jonathan, bringing the ark to Jerusalem, humility when disgraced by Absalom, extension of Israel's borders, the selection of Solomon to succeed him.

2. There are many obvious choices that illustrate a host of virtues evident in the life of David. In battle, he is brave; in dire straits, he is resourceful (even twice living with the Philistines!); in piety, he is sincere and inspirational; and interacting with prophets, he is teachable and humble. While it would hardly grab headlines or animate typical guy talk, it is worth considering David's greatest achievement to be his success in maintaining his humility and his stark self-awareness. David knew that he was but a creature and that God was Lord. And, most of the time, David lived accordingly.

3. A good answer to this question needs a good understanding of the two kinds of righteousness. A man lives in two distinct realities: his relationship with God, and his relationship with fellow creatures. What David does in this world's relationships does not win or affirm his relationship with God. Before God it is nothing but grace, pure and simple. But, before creatures, it is all about personal performance and effort. It is empty humility that enables one to stand (actually, fall prostrate!) before God. That David lived with this humility may be the best explanation for his lofty title.

4. The prose is painfully terse. No insight into David's thinking is offered. Several facts are worth consideration. David was in his Jerusalem residence while his general and army were besieging a

city. The king was idle, with time for afternoon naps and rooftop strolls. Nothing in the text implicates Bathsheba in any wrongdoing (don't assume immodesty—David's vantage might have provided a glimpse through a window). David was not afraid to use his position to satisfy his desire. Considered in light of David's harem, this sin indicates a significant struggle with the problem of lust.

5. This is a lengthy text, but since it is often overlooked and abounds with important lessons, it deserves attention. The story rings of authenticity: the details of each plot, those implicated in the execution, the wild shift of passions, the insidious work of lust, anger, vengeance, and the dynamics of family relationships all make the story real to us. Only Tamar displays pious zeal and wisdom. Certainly, hereditary sin is at work again. Abraham's penchant for deception was manifest in his progeny. David's lust is apparent in Amnon. Perhaps David's own sin with Bathsheba shamed him into silent inaction when Amnon followed his evil example.

6. The goal is to encourage the group to explore the role that David should have, or at least could have, played in the lives of his children. It is possible that some will make an argument meant to mitigate the weight of David's culpability. But it is important that participants come to recognize the serious responsibility of a father and the terrible suffering that can result when a father abdicates his role for any reason—even a legitimate one. Being human, we can always make an excuse for what we failed to do, and thus sins of omission become extremely difficult to acknowledge and own, even (or maybe especially) in our own lives.

7. Though it is not particularly pleasant, nothing is learned if we refuse to name David's domestic delinquency as sin. This is not meant to disparage the man's reputation (that is secure, as it rests in the reality of God's grace toward David), but to help fathers avoid his errors. Unfortunately, the reality of negligent fathering is epidemic yet today—even in the homes of solid Christian men. A desire to be kind, a fear of being similarly implicated, and a refusal to expect too much of fathers all fuel our tendency to ignore or excuse fatherhood failure.

8. This seems to be a hazard especially for those involved in some form of work within the Church. While sinful in themselves, whispered stories, with the obligatory raised eyebrows, about the

pastor's kids are a commonplace. A case could be made that in light of his own tragic experience—and the eventual cost of a nation in civil war—David might be an ardent champion of the importance of investing in family. Especially when children are young, there is no substitute for the gift of time.

9. That the Messiah would be descended from David, Israel's greatest, reminds us that even a fallen man and a father with many failings can be used within God's plan to accomplish much. One can learn from David and evaluate his life lessons, but charity toward the man and gratitude for his life should prevail. The Messiah is David's son by blood; every Jew in Jesus' day knew this. What was not expected, though explicit in David's own psalm (110:1), was that the Messiah would surpass David and be his Lord. Jesus is Lord, and He is the Davidic king, a name he did not despise, though bearing the divine name itself.

10. Fatherhood is always an exercise in grace. David, the great man of God who could yet fail so utterly in his responsibilities at home, should serve as warning to every man never to presume on his successes or to judge harshly the failures of another. Humble and circumspect living is ever the order of the day—particularly when it comes to exercising the critical work of a father.

# Job

1. This question will likely spark some pleasant memories of humorous childhood queries. But it may also prove a bit sobering, as children sometimes probe for answers to the same sort of existential questions that perplex us as adults: Why did a pet have to die? Why did God allow some disaster to strike? Why am I here? It is probably true that adults ask as many questions as children, only children have yet to learn that asking such questions aloud generates more perplexity and awkwardness than answers.

2. No doubt, the immediate crises of life will dominate the answers to this question. Illness, death, and tragedy may prompt some rather pointed and painful questions. Behind most of these, and present in most men who think, are the standard existential questions. (The term *existential* is meant not in its narrow use as a philosophical school, but generally—the sort of questions that surface simply by virtue of existing in this broken world.) These are the big questions, such as: Why was I born? What's the meaning of life? Why is there a universe? Why does God allow evil? What's the point of being good if we all die anyway?

3. Christians, steeped in salvation by grace through faith alone, often find these descriptions of Job utterly mystifying. A sinner by birth and action, he *can't* be blameless! This is a great instance of the two kinds of righteousness. It is true that before God (vertical righteousness), no man is justified apart from grace through faith. In fact, Job demonstrates precisely this humble faith when he yields to God's counter-questions and repents. Job is righteous and upright in his life among his fellow creatures (horizontal righteousness) because he is doing consistently what is required of him. The dilemma of the story is that a good man (horizontal righteousness) can still reap evil—in spite of the usual rules to the contrary.

4. It is significant that when God arrives to answer Job's challenge, He doesn't say, "Yeah, well, sorry about all of this, Job;

Satan doubted my assessment of your character, and I decided to prove him wrong. Good job!" In other words, the interchange between God and Satan is not the explanation for Job's (or anyone's) suffering. Nor is Job's ordeal a test to discover Job's real character—God already knew that. The text gives no "why?" answer.

5. Job is right. God is the ultimate source of his suffering. Satan may have sent the suffering, but God is complicit by allowing it. This is hard, and goes to the heart of the problem addressed in the book. Luther reminds us that Satan is "God's devil." It is cold comfort to blame Satan when God is still in charge and gives him space to operate. Whether the cause is God or Satan, in the end, the problem is the same. The only solution is to cling to God's promise of grace made certain and concrete in Christ.

6. Intriguing as the deep questions might be, it is good to return to the immediate and real issue of fatherhood. Participants should consider several of the ways that Job made an impact on his kids. Certainly, this list would include things specified in the text, such as his practice of interceding for his children and his decision to include his daughters in the inheritance. But participants should also be encouraged to consider Job's role as an example of faithful and upright living, an influence that is implicit in the text.

7. Christians should not offer sacrifices for their kids—yes, this includes not giving gifts of charity in their name in hopes of gaining some benefit for those children. However, they should pray regularly for their children, and those prayers should include every conceivable concern. Many parents rightly begin praying for a pious and upright spouse for their infant children. Obviously, petitions for spiritual faithfulness and maturity should also find a regular place in the prayers of parents for their children. Whatever contributes to the eternal welfare and earthly usefulness of a child is worthy of inclusion in a parent's prayer.

8. Clearly, our trust in the efficacy of prayer founded on God's promise to hear and answer our prayers gives us confidence that our praying makes a real difference for the welfare of our children. Equally difficult to measure, but also significant and worthy of consideration, is the fact that an active life of prayer affects the thinking of the one doing the praying and, in this case, helps to remind the parent of the importance of God's will at work directing

their child-rearing as well as highlighting the priority of spiritual and eternal realities as they make decisions for their children.

9. Integrity and consistency are perhaps the two most important words in successful parenting—yes, even more important than love and encouragement. A father who confesses and practices the same thing with consistency is living with integrity. When he calls on his children to do the same, they have reason to believe that this is a way of life worthy of their own emulation—the proof is the life of their own father. It is difficult to overestimate the significance of a father's moral and spiritual life and integrity for the sort of children that he raises. Members of the group can probably offer concrete examples of this from their own experience.

10. Underneath both the Easter text of Job 19 and the humble confession of the creature in Job 40 is the same unwavering faith that Job has in the promises and provision of his God. He knows his God, and with the help of God's answer Job is reminded of his relationship to his God: he is only a creature. His task is to trust, and such trust will *not* be disappointed. Answers that are intellectually satisfying might be hard to find in the story of Job, but the final answer is the best. God is God and His creatures can trust Him to make all things right. In Christ, this is our reality.

# Solomon

1. The question should stimulate some quick and nonthreatening discussion that ideally will progress into more meaningful reflection on exactly what constitutes wisdom or its practice. Help participants identify the characteristics or qualities present in those people that they consider to be wise.

2. Solomon displays a number of admirable character traits and virtues. He is pious, worshiping, loving, and obeys God (1 Kings 3:3). (The concession that he worshiped on the high places is hardly significant since the Jerusalem temple had yet to be built, as noted in verse 2.) Solomon values his father's legacy and appreciates his own privileged position (v. 6). Solomon is humble and appropriately self-deprecating, altogether aware of his own limitations (v. 7–9). And Solomon is wise, recognizing discernment and capacity to lead as his real needs. Taken all together, Solomon appears a remarkable man with admirable character.

3. A thorough study of Ecclesiastes lies beyond the scope of this chapter, but is too intriguing to ignore completely. Some may react quite negatively to what they see as the pessimism of these verses. Others may see them as reasonable advice in light of the text's unflinching assessment of life's bitterness and injustices. It is even possible to see within these verses a stirring call to embrace life and to celebrate the gifts of the day since they derive from God. The text is not endorsing an "eat, drink, and be merry" hedonism. Quite the contrary, Ecclesiastes 9:7 makes clear that once one's works have been "approved"—that is, once one is certain that his activity is within the bounds of God's revealed will (His Law), he is free to delight in what he is given to do and what he is given to enjoy. The Christian can follow this advice as he rejoices in the justification which is his in Christ and busies himself with what God has provided.

4. Some personalities struggle with this issue more than others. There are circumstances, however, that test the outlook of even the most optimistic. It is worth discussing the appropriate place of pessimism or even mild cynicism within the Christian faith. Even those eager to defend world-weariness and pessimism as compatible with faith need to recognize and concede the real danger of negativity that breeds despair—the loss of faith through an inability to trust anyone, including God. When cynicism reigns, hope dies. Of course, religion and faith are two different things. One may wonder about religion without rejecting God.

5. The group might want to discuss the polygamy issue. Remember that God's plan is one man and one woman in one marriage (Genesis 2:24; 1 Timothy 3:2). More pertinent is recognition of the primacy of the marriage relationship for a man's life. A man becomes "one flesh" with his wife—her influence is profound. And the example a man offers his children of Christ-like care for his bride (Ephesians 5:25–33) is differently but equally profound.

6. One could pick virtually any portion of Proverbs' first nine chapters, and the theme would be the same. Wisdom is much more than intellectual horsepower, or even savvy "street cred." Wisdom is closely allied with the ancient virtue of prudence—the ability to accurately assess any situation and arrive at an advantageous course through that situation. In the Bible, this wisdom always presumes a foundation of morality, that is, a life that strives to conform to God's will in every circumstance. In many ways, wisdom is living according to the Law of God, summarized nicely in the Decalogue.

7. Wisdom is mandatory for successful parenting. The idea here is to stimulate the group to consider the resources available. It is also expected that the participants might realize that not all experts on parenting are offering advice that is congruent with God's intention and direction for fatherhood. Obviously, "the Bible" is not a bad answer, but respondents should be pressed to be specific about what part of the Bible they have in mind. Ideally, those present should be able to identify men they know who are actually living models of the kind of fatherhood that upholds and honors God's purposes.

8. The question raises some interesting issues about the role of wisdom in a Christian's life. While admittedly open for debate, a

convincing case could be made that Solomon's confidence in his own wisdom created trouble for him—ignoring warnings and multiplying wives, cultivating realism and pessimism to the brink of despair, perhaps even trusting his own wit more than God's Word. Human wisdom is a great gift when conformed to God's will, but it must always be subservient to faith and simple trust in the promises and guidance of God. Some would argue that any neglect of God is by definition antithetical to true wisdom.

9. As indicated in the last answer, wisdom that ignores the essential place of God is an imposter and no longer qualifies as wisdom. Intellectualism and rationalism are exceedingly susceptible to deforming forces that make these human achievements guides and authorities without norm. In other words, they supplant God and become the final arbiters of what is true and right. When they claim this definitive role, they have arrogated to themselves God's place and become idols. Science in the modern world is frequently forced out of its legitimate and worthy pursuits and given status as virtually divine—a work for which it is woefully unqualified. Science is marvelous tool, but a miserable deity.

10. Like the bulk of the proverbs, this familiar text is best understood as descriptive of a general truth, and not as an ironclad promise. As we know, the way a child turns out is usually highly predictable if one takes into account the child's upbringing. Considered in this light, perhaps the case of Rehoboam is not anomalous. The best insurance of a successful faith handoff is a father who practices his faith with integrity and consistency and openly and routinely shares this practice with his children.

# Joseph

1. The group could take this question in a number of directions, any of which are fine. The goal is to stimulate some thinking about what it is that makes a father a father. Encourage the group to consider some of the qualities or characteristics that are essential for a father to succeed in his work.

2. The fact that Joseph was raising God's Son—indeed God Himself in the flesh—can cut both ways. There would have been advantages: Jesus could be counted on to be truthful, respectful, and always perfectly obedient. Joseph would not need to worry about behavior issues or about providing sufficient ethical guidance. On the other hand, the reality that he was responsible for the care of the Messiah could well have been a weight that sorely burdened Joseph—without relief. It would also be reasonable to assume that Joseph was prone to live rather circumspectly, knowing that his life was under the direct gaze of his Lord. Of course, this is true of us all, though we may be inclined to forget the fact.

3. "He sure seems normal. When will He start looking like a Messiah? What kind of power does He have? I wonder what He's thinking?" Such might have been Joseph's musings. A bit more reflection might have raised fascinating Christological quandaries: Jesus is obedient to His parents, yet they are obedient to His will established at creation. Joseph teaches Jesus to plane a board, yet Jesus created the wood that they shape. Joseph takes his son to the temple to worship God, but the temple was built for his Son. Of course, Joseph probably would not have realized the full import of all of this. Jesus' full identity as true God was revealed slowly, even to the disciples.

4. There are many unusual parts of the story: Mary and Joseph didn't notice Jesus' absence, it took three days to find him, Jesus was able to dialogue with the Jewish scholars, Jesus lives in "subjection" to His parents. That Jesus' comment about His

Father's house went over their heads indicates a normal family environment. Daily life must have been unremarkable, with Joseph playing the role of father quite naturally. There weren't overtones of "Hey! We're raising the Son of God!" Since Jesus is sinless, He did not disobey when He stayed in Jerusalem; as always, any worry was the sole fault of the worrier.

5. When God directs, people need to obey—instantly. In Joseph's case, delayed obedience could have spelled disaster for his young family. One of Joseph's greatest character traits is his willingness to do what he was asked to do without first demanding an explanation or time to think it over. Joseph understood that disciples simply do what needs to be done—reasonableness is not a factor. God continues to expect much of fathers. A father never outgrows obedience. In many ways, his burden to obey increases as he leaves childhood and grows into the responsibilities of fatherhood.

6. There is no way of knowing why Joseph never has any lines in the Bible. Perhaps it is a mark of his personality—the strong, silent type. Perhaps it is but a reflection of the basic male penchant for minimal verbiage. Regardless of his inclinations, a father needs to learn to speak appropriately. Some must learn to restrain what is too often a torrent of increasingly meaningless words, and more need to recognize the frequently occurring occasions when a father's words are essential. Even more important than the frequency of speaking, however, is the content and worth of what is said.

7. Certainly there are many responsibilities of a father, and obsession with one at the expense of the others is wrong. However, a certain primacy adheres to the responsibility of providing protection. When children are safe, then it is possible to address the other important tasks involved in raising them. In general, men seem to have mastered the art of getting distracted—usually the distractions are legitimate concerns and worthy tasks. The perennial danger is that important things overwhelm and supersede the *most* important things. Work, hobbies, recreation, sports, serving others, and serving at church can all become problems when they interfere with a man's most important responsibility: his own family.

8. We are usually quick to indict the decadent culture that inundates our children with images, ideas, icons, and encourage-

ment that are directly opposed to the standards established by the Creator. This is a real threat, but so is the threat of our own sinful flesh and our own self-serving proclivities. Life on a commune or in a cabin in the wilderness offers attractive solutions . . . but God calls us to engage the world. This question will likely spark a lively debate about permissive versus protective parenting. Sensitivity to personal situations of those in the group is in order, but a challenge to think about God's best for us is also fitting. A wise father will protect, yes, *shelter*, his children as much as possible for as long as possible, knowing that when well-formed in God's truth and reality, his children will, in time, be well-equipped to encounter every challenge of the culture.

9. Humility is simply seeing yourself honestly—as God sees you. It is impossible from the text to discern a leadership style in Joseph. However, he does nothing that would not fit with a spirit of genuine humility, and there are several indications that this was the case. Participants should be able to think of many great leaders that demonstrated humility. Whatever a man's vocation—leader or follower—an accurate self-assessment can only lead to humility. Strong leadership does not negate humility.

10. The study and the discussion about Joseph should provide ample suggestions regarding fatherhood responsibilities that would benefit from fresh attention. Encourage the participants to consider what would bring the most benefit to those for whom they are responsible: wife, children, grandchildren. Of course, even those who aren't fathers should be able to recognize ways that the lessons of Joseph can be applied in their own lives.

# Jairus

1. As usual, the goal is simply to cultivate the flow of conversation and discussion. Participants may offer personal recollections from the view of either father or child, or they may even simply relate things they have heard about. Intentionally ambiguous, the question may prompt responses that range from disarming and humorous to quite sobering.

2. It is at least probable that Jairus had been an eyewitness to the synagogue healing of the paralytic and the demoniac before him (Mark 1:21–28). Jairus saw what Jesus could do. Given the new factor of acute personal need—a dying daughter—Jairus found all the motivation he needed. How one understands what constitutes faith determines the evaluation of Jairus' motive. Jairus did not confess Jesus as God in the flesh (at this point, not even the disciples were ready to do this); he may have had doubts about whether Jesus was Messiah, but he believed that Jesus could and would heal his daughter. He believed. He knew enough. The cry for Jesus' help is from faith.

3. That Jairus, the responsible party in the synagogue, actually would initiate a conversation with Jesus already puts him in an awkward spot with those among the religious elite who were opposed to Jesus. It is too easy for us to pigeonhole the various groups with finality: scribes and Pharisees = bad, Jesus and disciples = good. Jairus reminds us that it was not so easy to draw the lines and that individuals were sometimes caught with a line running through them. That Jairus falls at Jesus' feet to emphasize the humility and ardor of his appeal is all the more remarkable for a man of his statue. Of course, simple pride should not be overlooked—begging is never pleasant for any person.

4. As we have seen, David learned the truth of these words the hard way. His prideful sin finally collapsed in unconditional surrender to God's judgment. Jairus shows his own appreciation for this fact when he falls at Jesus' feet. He does not seek help—he

pleads for mercy. The greatest truth at work is that for Jairus, there was no option. His self-abasement before Jesus was the only thing he could do. It was not premeditated or calculated. The Christian life begins with God laying low the one He converts, that when He in mercy imputes faith, that faith receives God's mercy and holds it dear.

5. It should first be noted that most people probably refuse to believe this idea. The Christianity they have encountered requires no such humiliation—rather it promises to meet their every need and bring them the personal fulfillment they have sought elsewhere but not found. The reality is that sinners must die. They die under the devastating demands of the Law and, like Jairus, can only plead for mercy. People do not like this idea because it removes every shred of human dignity or worth from the equation of salvation. The fact is that God does it all, and we can only beg and receive what He gives—which is infinitely more than we ever could have dreamed in our limited human imagination.

6. That Jairus was anxious or even frantic about the interruption seems fair to surmise. On the other hand, there is no question about who was in control of this entire scenario. Jairus may have been leading the way, but Jesus was in fact leading Jairus to learn what he needed to learn: trust in Christ. Perhaps, in the presence of Jesus, Jairus actually identified and sympathized with the agonized woman. The waiting, the devastating news, the exhortation from Jesus, and Jairus' growing dependence on Jesus all teach him the way of faith.

7. From mourning to laughing—perhaps this indicates something about the lack of sincerity of this crowd of mourners (professional mourners were common). Or maybe it is simply hopeless, helpless humans persuading themselves that they are in control. People mock what they don't understand. Laughing at God and His ways cultivates an illusion of superiority. The laughter may have made Jairus wonder about the wisdom of throwing in his lot with Jesus, who was clearly not operating within the usual bounds of human rationality. The ridicule of peers (real or perceived) is a force more powerful than most of us realize or care to admit.

8. Pride is a force with far greater influence and power than most men are willing to recognize. Perhaps we are too accustomed to living with it as a present reality. The idea is to get the group to consider pride as a force that often determines our actions or

inactions and often keeps us from the best course with our parenting. Pride can manifest itself in a crippling concern over what others will think, in a refusal to risk feeling weird doing some activity, or in a smug assurance that men don't do that. All of these can be unyielding roadblocks that thwart God's plan for fatherhood.

9. The group will need to use their own experience and learning to supply answers to this question. Male self-sufficiency and fear of losing esteem with his peers are powerful forces in the lives of all men—not just adolescent males. Self-preservation instincts and pride can lead a man to neglect and even reject the needs of his children—be that the need to play dress-up with a five-year-old daughter or the need to apologize to a sixteen-year-old son.

10. One's life situation will shape the answer. The words can be heard either way. Worry and fear qualify as sin and call for repentance. And though it is cast in the imperative, "only believe' is pregnant with promise, and faith thrills at the words. When belief is in Jesus, there is no disappointment. What Jairus learned is still true: for Jesus, the finality of death is not final. Not every dying child will rise from her sickbed, but in Christ, all who die will rise to life.

# The Official

1. Apparently for some men, this is only a slight exaggeration—they have an intense aversion to seeking help when traveling. Other men surrender to another idol of masculinity—efficiency—and recognize getting input from local experts as a way to facilitate the speedy completion of a task. Many justifications can be offered, but a candid man who will not ask would admit that pride lies at the bottom of the refusal, just as it does for the man zealous for the quickest route to completion.

2. Even in two short verses, we gain significant information about this man. One could argue that his actions illustrate great love for his son; a humility that is willing to admit inability and seek help; an altruism willing to travel twenty miles to seek Jesus' help; a tenacity to repeat his request until it was acknowledged; and a confidence that Jesus was someone who could help his son. In short, simply by making the journey to Cana, the official from Capernaum demonstrates a number of virtues worthy of imitation.

3. Most often, *how* something is said communicates more than *what* is said. We don't know Jesus' tone or nonverbal language. We only have his words, which appear brusque and indifferent. The words could easily provoke offense, cause confusion, or simply discourage—why would Jesus say such a thing when a man is just trying to save his son's life? It hardly seems the ideal time for a lesson on true faith or an evaluation of the Galilean ministry's effectiveness. But Jesus' words have the desired effect: they push the man more deeply into the reality of faith in Christ and His word alone.

4. That translation is an inexact science is too often forgotten by readers of English Bibles. This discussion should lend greater appreciation for the sorts of difficult choices that often must be made in translation. The question is at what moment did the man move from a polite and desperate plea for help to a conviction of faith in the identity of Jesus? "Sir" is still waiting for faith to arrive.

"Lord" evidences the full bloom of faith in the person and work of Jesus. Most translators opt for the first position, but your group can feel free to make a case for the second option.

5. The official knew the standard rubrics for healing: lay on hands, say a prayer, speak the command of restoration. It was tried and true, and it was a pattern that Jesus often followed. But, Jesus was not bound by any norm or expectation. He healed people in a variety of ways: by touching (Mark 1:41), by spitting and making mud (John 9:6), by saying a word (as here), by saying nothing and only being touched (Mark 5:29). Each way accomplished healing, but more importantly, also accomplished something for the one receiving the healing. In this case, healing from a distance of twenty miles confirms the faith that Jesus desired in the official.

6. In the context of the story, it is exciting to see faith soar to new heights and the hard facts of a son hopelessly dying trod underfoot. It is altogether different when that same principle is turned on our modern world, when the empirical evidence is supported by the academic and intellectual elites who scoff at the superstitious notions of those who continue to profess faith in a God who creates, judges, redeems, and restores. This question can only be answered by another study, but the participants at least need to wrestle with the reality that faith and its expectations may well put them at odds with the rest of the world.

7. The first part of this question is pure conjecture since we are not told. It is likely that the official told his entire household about Jesus and shared with them His saving words, which they received through faith (Romans 10:17). For John, faith is the goal of the entire Gospel (John 20:31). That an entire household came to believe through one man's earnest encounter with Jesus and his faithful response is cause for celebration. Faith that yields eternal life is the true goal.

8. The group will likely have powerful anecdotes of positive as well as negative impacts. Either one make the same case that is consistently substantiated by statistics: a father has more impact on the faith of his children than any other adult. This should humble and embolden the men present and spark some earnest discussion about what one does with this power. Which tool is most effective is open for debate, but as indicated in the narrative, consistency and integrity arguably possess the greatest potential to secure an enduring legacy.

9. The official received faith from Jesus and learned to trust what God would give. This was a gift from God merely received by the official who could do nothing (as none of us can) to make it reality. On the other hand, the official's responsibility—to be faithful—was a task he needed to accomplish for the good of his family. God empowers this, of course, but it is the task of the man (and of every man) to carry out what God has given him to do. Clearly these two great realities, God's gift of saving faith and man's responsibility to be faithful, are quite distinct and not to be confused, yet vibrantly intertwined in the experience of the believer.

10. "A royal priesthood" is the astounding and magnificent title Peter applies to God's people (1 Peter 2:9). Hence, when he received faith, the royal official became a truly royal official—not by connection to a human monarchy, but through faith worked by the world's true King. All who follow Christ in faith bear the same title. By our union with the Lord, each one of us is, indeed, a royal—even if the paparazzi fail to appear.

# The Prodigal's Father

1. Clearly, this is a demanding question, but it can be steered in a less intimidating direction by starting with some childhood failures or disasters. First accident stories might be safely shared as well. Of course, if the group is comfortable with one another, the room should be given to those participants who may want to relate personal and even painful events. Be sure to explore with the group what it is that makes the experience of forgiveness so wonderful and powerful. Restoration of relationships, and relief from guilt will likely top the list.

2. While coming to one's senses may not always be a synonym for repentance, in this context it seems to be the case. The boy's rehearsed speech includes a confession of sin and an awareness of the breach of relationship he has caused. He knows that after his actions he won't be able to waltz back into his old life like nothing has changed. God works contrition and uses His Law to accomplish it. Such is the case here. The Law plagued the boy's conscience; the result of his disobedience was the unraveling and suffering of life pressing in on him. How the Gospel, the undeserved love of God in Christ, stands in sweet contrast!

3. Since not even the Bible adheres to this old principle of interpretation, it is wise not to be overzealous in its implementation. However, in Luke 15, it is clear that Jesus' point is to justify His reception of tax collectors and sinners—the lost. Any other conclusions derived from the parable are ill-advised at best since the parable is not meant to be a source of parenting principles. Misinterpretation could lead one to argue that parents can't say no; that one is not accountable for his bad behavior; and that parents should not prevent a child's wrong choice.

4. The brilliance of the parable is to leave none excluded from its message. In reality, the vagaries of life eventually put each of us in each role: absurdly wrong and needing forgiveness, upright and good and needing forgiveness, and called upon to offer forgiveness

to the penitent. The incredible aspects attach most of all to the father's inexplicable permissiveness—which should be seen as nothing more than a necessary but incidental plot device. Odd as this family may seem, experience assures us that Jesus' portrayal does not exceed the limits of credibility. The situation is immediately recognizable.

5. The "lostness" of the younger son is apparent. His older brother is equally lost—failing to delight in his father's love and refusing to acknowledge his own need for forgiveness and grace. This is always the danger that stalks those who live upright lives: success in life can obscure the universal need for grace. Gently, the father appeals to this son to see the truth of grace and its varying application to unique individuals. That a sinner receives grace should be a cause of joy, not offense. The Father, like every wise father, tailors His message to each child's need.

6. As the story begins, the father's odd behavior simply provides the circumstances that will allow the heart of the story to unfold—a rebellious son who repents and is received. While we should not obsess over the oddity of the father's lack of intervention to prevent his son's fall, we should not miss what is meant to shock because it is so audacious and so unbelievable. The father has amazing love, incredible grace, and unrestrained forgiveness. This is unreal. Grace always is. That's the point. God has that kind of grace; decent, merit-oriented man finds it grossly offensive and unacceptable.

7. Yes, this question is a bit out there. The point is that if one reads and studies simply to find principles or lessons for successful living, then the real beauty of the Gospel will be consistently obscured and forfeited. Certainly, the Bible contains lessons to be learned—the Law does have a positive place in the life of God's people. But when the text is actually delivering a message of grace, it dare not be lost by a frantic and foolhardy hunt for lessons. The lost son delivers grace. Each participant should experience it: God loves and chooses and receives *me*.

8. After that last question, a softball question seemed justified. But don't cheat and allow the group to spout "the Bible," and then move on. The idea is to get the group to identify and appreciate the means that God has established for the delivery of His grace and guidance. God does this when His Word is proclaimed: sermon, absolution, the Lord's Supper and private confession all become

critical points for delivering grace. That these tasks are the essential work of the Church should not be missed. Finally, the mutual encouragement of fellow believers is another precious gift used for God's purposes.

9. This is a problem that persistently besets Christians who delight in the truth of the Gospel. Forgiveness is not orderly or logical. It provides a poor structure for ethics or for training in righteousness. That is not its purpose! So while a father must be liberal in his delivery of the untamed Gospel, he must not use the Gospel as license. Forgiveness does not remove responsibility. Wild grace and careful instruction, unrestrained forgiveness and the expectation of increasing maturity, unconditional Gospel and the formation of character by habituation, these dualities must animate the Christian father in his work. Learning the balance is the work of a lifetime—dependent on its own regular reception of grace.

10. One cannot be dogmatic, of course, but it would be wonderful if participants might be able to articulate the difference between teaching the Gospel and receiving the Gospel. That's the point of this parable. One can merely learn the lesson: forgiveness is radical; my kids need to know this. Or one can find himself on the receiving end of the Gospel, delighting to know that the forgiveness of the parable's Father is forgiveness given to him. This is a truth to cherish and ponder for a lifetime.